# RADICAL
# JOY

# RADICAL JOY

## AWAKENING YOUR POTENTIAL FOR TRUE FULFILLMENT

TODD EVAN PRESSMAN, Ph.D.

# CONTENTS

# PART I

# BUILDING THE FOUNDATION

# THE CALL TO JOY

> Listen,—perhaps you catch a hint of an ancient state
> not quite forgotten; dim, perhaps, and yet not
> altogether unfamiliar, like a song whose name is long
> forgotten, and the circumstances in which you heard
> completely unremembered. . . . But you remember . . .
> how lovely was the song, how wonderful the setting
> where you heard it, and how you loved those who were
> there and listened with you. . . . The notes are
> nothing. Yet you have kept them with you . . . as a soft
> reminder of what would make you weep if you
> remembered how dear it was to you. . . . Listen, and see
> if you remember an ancient song you knew so long
> ago and held more dear than any melody you taught
> yourself to cherish since.
>
> —*A Course in Miracles*

Something deep within us stirs when we hear the call to Joy. We have heard it before, at peak moments in our lives, but have not answered. It is said, "The greatest tragedy in life is to die with your music still in you." Too often, we live out our "lives of quiet desperation," never tending to the song of the soul.

It is time to listen once again for the call to Joy, to put aside the daily grind and stop waiting for things to somehow change. It is time to start attending to the longing of our depths and the whispering of our hearts. It is time to return to who we truly are, remembering that only Joy is important in the end.

It has become "fashionable" to dismiss this call with the mistaken idea that real Joy is impossible. We are admonished against being unrealistic and building up false hopes. We plod along, dedicated only to keeping up with our routines, stealing a few moments of escape when we can.

In our conditioning to the everyday, we hypnotically follow the dictates of daily obligation. We have developed a philosophy of the ordinary, never looking beyond the tiny field of our immediate concerns. And in so doing, we shut out that which *is* important, that which answers the very basic and obvious questions: "Why am I doing these things? What is the purpose of my life?"

Asking such questions with honesty and humility is a first step toward finding answers. How would we convince ourselves this time to push away these questions, to avoid taking action on what really matters to us, to ignore the yearnings of our heart? It is time, indeed, to put aside the daily grind, to recognize where our ways are not working, and to start attending to "the music within," the call to Joy. What else, in the final accounting, is worthy of our lives and our dignity?

This book speaks to the tremendous power and freedom that comes with the discovery of true Joy, radical Joy. Such a discovery gives sweeping perspective on the problems of human existence, that we may uproot them at their very source. Striking at the core of our collective psyche and spirit, we reveal the essence of pain and Joy, opening the way to a new strategy for living, one where our every action converges on the pathway "Home."

The quest for Joy, then, is not a matter of managing each of our problems and attempting to win over them, but truly transcending them, even dissolving them, as a higher reality swallows them up. Rather than pushing arduously against the world, we may flow gracefully into our Good. Everything conspires toward this aim, and we will not be satisfied until we have reached our mark.

What is radical Joy? It is more than the transient happiness of the world, happiness which in its transience can give way to loss, pain, and disappointment. Radical Joy is the discovery of high Purpose, ultimate Meaning, and deep Fulfillment.

Such a discovery comes as we let go of the age-old struggle to change reality to suit our liking, and embrace the whole of it just as it is. With this, we see how perfect is the design of our human experience, and find meaning in its every detail. All opposites are reconciled in a great unity. We are released from suffering and dance with the infinite variety of life.

The living experience of radical Joy can best be conveyed by example. The following quotations of several people with whom I have worked are but a small sampling. While names and certain details have been changed for purposes of confidence, these are real people living in the real world.

Susan, a 44-year-old librarian, came to see me for a paralyzing fear of rejection and abandonment. In a meeting one day, while rehearsing what she might say to sound "important and interesting," she saw the fear behind this tactic and caught it as it was forming:

> I could see where my mind was running. I was consciously noticing that I was afraid and [began] stepping back from my fear and letting myself be. And it was like I had an altered experience. I literally felt myself being lifted out of ego into some other plane and I started blissing out. I felt incredible love. I looked back at [my friend sitting next to me] and felt such love and harmony, and all the rest of it just fell away. [The fear] was like these little specks of dirt that you could just brush away, compared to this magnificent way, the "Spirit" way, of looking at things.

John, a 39-year-old realtor, upon achieving a higher perspective, described it this way:

> I see now that everything we always worry about in life is going to be okay, that it's all part of a learning process helping us come to this absolute certainty that everything's leading to . . . our growth and it's all okay. There's

nothing to be afraid of or upset by or worried about. *It's all okay!*

Janet, a 50-year-old schoolteacher and mother with debilitating lupus, came to a deeper understanding of the suffering in her life and how to deal with it:

I keep having these overwhelming feelings of what the human condition is all about. All the fear and constriction and angst we go through here. And then the understanding that it's all so beautiful, really, behind it all. I keep thinking, if only we could remember this feeling, if only we could remember. I have a strong desire to help people remember that it's all beautiful, and they shouldn't worry, that everything is just fine behind it all.

Steven, a 42-year-old construction worker who was severely debilitated after 18,000 volts of electricity ran through him during a work accident, transcended his suffering and said:

Somewhere along the line I realized that even though I can't use my body anymore, I have something more than what I had before the accident. There is a peace in me that nothing can take away, and no matter what the limits of my body, I know that life holds incredible riches and discovery in the littlest of things. It's all a great big adventure!

And Frank, a 53-year-old maintenance worker, who was caught in the explosion of a hot water heater with boiling water scalding him almost to the point of death, said:

Having faced death, moving back and forth through the door between this world and the next, when I finally made a decision to come back to this world, I lost all my fear. Having lived through the worst of it all, nothing could scare me now. I can take things as they come and as they go. I don't worry about the future, about holding on to security, and all that. Mind you, I don't shy away from life, not at all. I'm living it more fully now, in each moment, you know? That's the gift of not having fear.

Ordinary people discovering an extraordinary fact: That Joy, *radical* Joy, is possible no matter what the limits of circumstance. These kinds of transformations can be readily achieved . . . they are neither mystical nor random. With right understanding and dedicated application, we can break free from what Michelangelo called "the statue in the stone," into the discovery of who we truly are.

For there is something in the spirit that yearns for full expression. To reinvoke a sense of wonder, to celebrate the miracle of being Alive! Radical Joy is the natural result of releasing this spiritual something from a lifetime of encrusted fears and repressions. The soul emerges like an oyster revealing its pearl, and we stand in the presence of the miraculous, new and lustrous, wide-eyed with wonder.

Within our means is the ability to pinpoint the very sources of suffering and then to release them, finding a natural flow and ease that leads us to our Good. That which the world needs most to know is that real Joy is possible. We simply need the tools to realize it in the everyday circumstances and challenges of our lives.

This book is a road map by which we may travel this path. It is an x-ray view into the psyche, with powerful methods for living a life of radical Joy. Together, we will discover the essence of what it is to be human, the source of our sufferings, and the discovery of a profound and transcending Fulfillment.

As you will notice, the book is part descriptive and part prescriptive, reflecting the twin aspects of any good path for growth: insight and action. The descriptive sections give a penetrating exploration of what makes for Joy and suffering. We will develop a vigorous and challenging insight into the nature of our struggles, the beliefs which underlie them, and the perceptual reality which springs forth from them. The essential cause of conflict, whether in our relationships, in our institutions, or within ourselves, will be revealed to point the way to the release from pain and the true experience of Joy. Compelling stories from the lives of the Buddha, St. Francis, Jesus, Gandhi, Mother Teresa, and the everyday man and woman bring these ideas to life. Like the Zen koans, paradox often becomes the means through which the ego is boggled, and the way to higher revelation paved.

The exercises of the book constitute the "how to" of Joy. They take these principles out of abstraction and into the arena of our lives. Without this, they would remain as nice ideals, inspiring perhaps, but ineffective against the nitty-gritty challenges we face. The exercises offer a comprehensive program to transcend the marketplace of misery and arrive at a truly radical Joy.

We will walk through three "doorways of transformation"— the doorways of the mind, body, and spirit—to enter into the realms of high Joy.

In the "doorway of the mind," we will unravel the "core fear," the distorting lens through which we interpret the world, the fundamental obstacle to our Joy. With such insight, the "what to do about it" becomes obvious and our journey to Joy the inevitable result.

In the "doorway of the body," we will look at the ways in which our bodies become the screens upon which psychic pain is projected into physical form. Exercises are given to break up these "emotional cysts," so that the body may instead become a vehicle for Joy.

In the "doorway of the spirit," our work is about transcendence, transcendence of our "littleness" and transcendence of the separate sense of self, as we are lifted "above the battleground." The meditations of the mystics, the ecstatic practices of the Sufis, the mindfulness of Buddhism—these are some of the ways by which we will rise into Joy.

These ingredients are then pulled together in the Vision quest. Examining all of the areas of our lives, we are empowered to begin living our Vision *now*, turning obstacles into opportunities and releasing ourselves to stand in a world of limitless possibilities. In so doing, we discover that our greatest suffering has become our most valuable teacher. No one is better equipped or more intimately experienced than we are to help transform the difficulties we have struggled with for so long. This, then, prescribes a Vision, a guiding mission for leading our journey onward. The tools are given so that this Vision may take root in the real world and grow to its ultimate fruition. The result is a life of ever-increasing Wonder, transcendent Beauty, and high Purpose—radical Joy!

And so, the tone is set for an experience that will not be mere armchair philosophizing, but a rigorous, sometimes demanding, and always exciting journey toward Fulfillment. Let us begin.

# CHAPTER 1

# THE PATHWAY TO JOY: FINDING AND FACING OUR FEARS

One does not become enlightened by imagining figures of light but by making the darkness conscious.

—C. G. Jung

Early in his career, St. Francis of Assisi had a terrible fear of lepers. One day, while riding his horse, a leper appeared in the path before him, blocking his way. Francis was paralyzed. In a peak of panic, his consciousness opened up. He got off his horse, as if moved by a higher Hand, and walked toward the leper. Trembling, he kissed him on the lips. With this he became filled with an overwhelming sweetness, immersed in a divine bliss. He bowed his head and closed his eyes, seeing the face of the Beloved in his mind. Upon opening his eyes, the leper was nowhere to be found.

This beautiful story reveals a great secret: When we find and face our fear, we are flooded with a Joy that has always been waiting for us. For Francis, the leper held the key to this secret. But he was not available to discover it while, in his fear, he kept running away. When we find and face our fear, it loses all power. When we meet our fear head-on, a sleeping giant awakens in us—we realize there must be something in us "bigger" than the fear, something ennobling, something joyous and magnificent, that has the power to stand up to it. And in standing up to it, we see the gold it hid all the while.

The answer to understanding our human condition and rising above it into Freedom is found in this dance between Joy and fear. Anger, guilt, loneliness, anxiety, boredom—these are some of the many faces of fear. At its foundation, fear threatens to take away our sense of safety and wholeness. We spend our lifetimes building massive walls of protection and insanely complicated strategies to defend against this. We are never free; we must always be alert to the prospect of a new attack, our forces of defense readied.

We carry the burden of this in our minds, perceiving the signs of threat everywhere. We carry it in our bodies as well—all pain and sickness spring forth from these maneuvers. And we suffer the greatest deprivation of all . . . the loss of spirit, the forgetting of the ideals of Purpose and Meaning. All this is spawned by the belief in fear, the belief that "something out there" threatens to take away our Joy.

The great discovery of the path to Joy is that fear is but an assumption, and a faulty one at that. It is an inaccurate way of understanding who we are and what reality is. It is not given in the nature of things. It is, rather, a way of looking at the world which assumes it to be threatening and hides its Joy. Original perception does not see fear; this layer gets added through life experience and conditioning. The good news, then, is that we may remove such conditioning, peeling away the assumptions of fear, to rediscover the Joy that it had kept in hiding. All that is needful is to find and face our fear.

## Exposing the Lie of Fear

There are two ways in which finding and facing fear disarms it. First, if a fear cannot make us run from it, then we realize there must be something in us more powerful than the fear, something that is capable of standing up to it. The fear cannot be the dreaded thing we always imagined. This realization is its own reward, giving us the courage to take on life and live it fully.

Yet there is an even greater surprise waiting for us when we confront our fear: We discover that *it is not real.* Only by avoiding it can we continue to believe there must indeed be something to fear. Turning around to take a look at what is actually chasing us, we find that it is not at all what we had thought.

At worst, we find a problem which we now can understand. And in understanding it, we see opportunities for transforming the problem, opportunities which were always there but which remained invisible while we wore the blinders of fear. As long as we avoid our fear, turning our heads away in horror of *the idea* of what it must look like, we blow it up into monstrous proportions. When finally we dare to take a look at what we have been running from, we find it is but a mouse that roared, casting huge and gruesome shadows on the wall.

Often, upon facing our fear, we discover that the entire illusion was made up! With eyes tightly shut as we go flailing about in the dark, we imagine a terror that has no substance at all. The simple act of opening our eyes, looking at what we were so certain was fearful, exposes the lie for what it is.

To give a new twist to an old fable, the voice of our fear is like the boy who cries wolf. He evokes our automatic, fearful response each time he creates images of the terrifying wolf in our minds, until finally we get wise to him—we get tired and bored of its empty threats—realizing at last that the fear has no bite. In truth, the wolf never comes, for he was made up of the stuff of our fear, a fantasy having no real power to carry out its threat.


## "This, Too, Shall Pass"

Fear *always* gives way to freedom and to Joy. For the one high truth that no fear can stand up to is that fear is imperma-nent; only Joy is enduring. In the end, all fears must pass and lose their power. That which threatens cannot threaten forever without eventually becoming commonplace and uninterest-ing. If it does strike, even if it does its worst to us, eventually it is forgotten. We learn the important lesson "This, too, shall pass."

Again, the problem is that we fail to face our fear, to test our assumption that it holds terrible consequences. Fear throws up the images of these consequences before our eyes and we stop dead in our tracks, blindly obeying its dictates, never proceeding to see if the threat is real. We become immobilized by frightening images of what will happen should we defy it. We become transfixed by these images, mesmerized by their awesome power, endlessly reciting the old, tireless dirge "I must protect and defend myself." In the instant we are con-fronted with fear, all free choice seems to fly out the window as we are compelled to react defensively.

In our paralysis, we fail to ask the all-important question "What happens next?" after the immediate consequences of fear pass. Such a question inevitably leads us to realize that the devastation fear promised is not permanent, and the idea that it would destroy us is not realistic.

We have spent our lives fixated upon fear. Enamored of its glittery horror, we keep looking at it with a kind of terrible fascination. We watch for its subtlest move, anticipating where and how it will strike next, utterly devoted to keeping safe from it. And until we look through this "sensuous" disguise to the other side of fear, we will not discover that we have a choice in this, a choice in how we want to relate to and create our lives.

Our avoidance of fear and our failure to test its assumptions means that we will continue assuming them. For no real experience comes along to challenge the belief. Indeed, we can strengthen our fear by this tactic, deciding that there must be something quite awful that is keeping us from even looking at it.

But when we do dare to look at it with the detachment of our observing selves, playing out the scenario to see what happens next, it eventually transforms. Perhaps we get tired of living under fear's rule, becoming bored with its endless tirade. Or perhaps we become interested in finally being done with the game and start looking for freedom and happiness. Either way, when we realize that "this, too, shall pass," we can release ourselves from the assumptions of fear that had been running our lives.

## Discovering the Power to Choose

What makes it hard to face fear, to trust that it is not what it seems, is that we actually *choose* to be afraid. We choose to put our attention on fear, believing that if we keep a watchful eye out for possible signs of danger, we will stay safe and preserve our Joy. This strategy requires that we focus exclusively on the fear, and never look to the other side to see either that it will pass or that it is not real at all.

How do we play out this strategy? First, we make up the thoughts of what might go wrong in a particular situation and assume that these thoughts are accurate. We then invest our belief in these assumptions, energizing them with our attention. We literally bring them to life by looking for signs to verify that they are real. An innocent statement by a friend is misinterpreted as a criticism; an oversight by our boss is taken as neglect. We pick out those features of a situation that confirm our fearful assumptions, zeroing in on them to the exclusion of the rest.

Next, we react to these signs as if they indeed hold the threat we anticipated. Our reaction becomes the "proof" that the fear was real, that there was something real compelling us to react. It is at this point that we fail to look further, to inquire whether these signs of threat are real or not. And so we stop, put up our defenses, shut our eyes and ears against the situation, and resolve to keep it away. Each step of this process is a willful choice.

We have been energizing our belief in fear this way our entire lives. The power of this constant repetition, this self-brainwashing, is such that the fear we originally dreamt up seems very real indeed. The certainty with which we believe our fear is real is evidence for how thoroughly we have practiced it. For when we walk through the fear and see that it is not what we thought, we are forced to admit we must have made it up.

Our fear, then, is a mirage, with all the appearances of reality, trying to force us to turn back and give up our search for Joy. But armed with the understanding that we "made it up," realizing that it has never really worked as a strategy for finding Joy, we can begin to test its assumptions. We can begin to open the door where fear says "Do not enter." The many threats we may hear as we do so—some subtle, some obvious—are simply the leftovers from our years of habit in which we assumed the fear was real. Steadily, even confidently, we walk straight through these hallucinations, empty ghosts of ideas that we once chose and never challenged. With each step we discover that the fear can do no harm, and we walk out of our imaginary prison cell and into the true meaning of Freedom.

We always have the power to choose Joy over fear. What we put our attention on is up to us. If someone asks you to think "apple," you can conjure up a picture in your mind of an apple. If someone then asks you to think "orange," you can choose to change that picture in your mind and think of an orange. A simple shift in attention, shining the spotlight of awareness first on one idea, then another. There is no "order of difficulty" in this; one is not scarier or harder to think of than the other. Again, it is simply a matter of where we place our attention.

It is the same with fear or Joy. A joyful idea is not harder to think of than a fearful one. The only thing that makes it difficult to choose Joy is our continued investment in fear as a strategy for staying safe. We must see that, not only does this strategy fail to make us truly safe, but it also keeps us ever-afraid, separate from Joy. Running from fear in the hope of escape actually preserves the problem, infusing it with life. It keeps us forever on a treadmill, the fear just behind us all the time. We must get wise to this, recognizing the illusion of fear, and "choose once again."

Where we place our attention—on fear or Joy—*is* up to us. The key to this discovery is to face our fear, challenging its assumptions and finding that it is not at all what we had imagined. With this, we see that fear is really a constellation of assumptions we have chosen, locking us into the picture of a fearful world. In facing our fear and exposing it as an illusion, we will find it has no real power to limit Joy.

## Right or Happy?

The question of whether radical Joy is possible boils down to the question of whether we prefer being right or happy. Do we want to protect and defend and justify our fears, or do we want to find Joy? In our strategy to avoid fear, we have taught ourselves to prefer being right with the idea that it provides security, predictability, and the fulfilling of what is expected of us—the trademarks of a life lived in fear. When we see, after years of heartache and no fulfillment, that we were wrong, we righteously defend our position, having invested so much of ourselves, indeed our very identities, in this approach.

Not looking to the other side of fear's consequences leads

to great suffering as we stop ourselves from fully living, to stay "safe," "secure," and "comfortable." We then work to convince ourselves we have made the right choice and eventually forget that there was a choice at all. "That's just how life is," we are told, and then internalize the message to make it our own. But this is the teaching of those who have made such a choice and, not wanting to be faced with their own ambivalence, would convert others in order to build a consensus.

All of us are coming to Joy. Life, in confronting us with our fears, will see to that. The more vigorously we take on life and gather experiences, the more quickly we learn the lesson. As we encounter our fears, sooner or later it occurs to us that they are an empty boast. We get bored with their posturing, jaded with the same old response of defending ourselves "just in case," fed up with living scared all the time and "sick and tired of being sick and tired." If we attempt to hide from life, if we try to stay too "safe," we only prolong the inevitable confrontation with fear, and postpone the discovery that it is not real.

Let us not delay but speed up the time of this discovery, pulling the plug on fear. Let us say, as Trudy the baglady said, "I refuse to be intimidated by reality." Let us begin to actively pursue, find, and face our fears.

When we do so, at first with the faith that these ideas make sense, and later with accumulated experience that proves their validity, a huge energy is unleashed within us. This is the energy that had been bound up throughout a lifetime, keeping vigil over our fears lest they spring forth and attack us when we are unaware. It is the energy we knew as children, before fear took charge of our lives. This energy reverses the aging process—literally—and guides us intuitively in all our decisions. It is the wellspring for the Joy which informs and infuses each moment of life.

Like drawing back the curtain from the booth in *The Wizard of Oz*, we can at last reveal the mystery of pain and Joy. They are understood as the workings of the choicemaker within, behind the curtain, pulling the levers and turning the dials of our perception. Recognizing this, we see that our lives are not determined by experiences out of our control. *We* set the agenda; *we* can change it at any moment. This is freedom, the freedom to express our Life Impulse, without the constraints of circumstance. Only in this is real Fulfillment, radical Joy, possible.

True freedom is not arranging circumstances to suit our wishes; this can never succeed. It is, rather, the ability to say "yes" to all things that life presents us, to dance gracefully with them. Finding and facing our fear is the key. When we do so, we unveil the great secret the world is looking for: that nothing, *nothing,* has the power to disturb our peace or limit our Joy in any way. We are not the victims of the world we see. We are its creators, its directors, and ultimately, its lovers.

## Jennifer

I would like to offer a real-life story to show how possible all of this is. This is the journey of one woman who had the courage to face her fear, to face herself, and in so doing, find her Joy.

Jennifer was 34 years old when an associate of mine first saw her in the hospital. She had just suffered a devastating back injury and a series of medical complications that left her paralyzed from the waist down. All of her dreams for the future were taken away from her, cruelly, in a matter of months. She would talk to no one.

My associate, a psychiatrist, was invited to see her by the attending physician, who recognized the signs of her withdrawal from life. On his first visit to her hospital room, he saw a young woman with a sweet and innocent face. Her long brown hair fell down to her shoulders. But he had to see this through a dark cloud. Not only would she not talk to him, she would not even look up. Finally, after repeated and unsuccessful attempts to find a way "in," she said "You're a psychiatrist, aren't you?" When he replied that he was, she made it clear she wanted to have nothing to do with him.

The next day, on a pure whim, he copied a page from a favorite spiritual book for her and, without saying a word, dropped it on her bed. He left the room. The day after that, he dropped off another page and again said nothing. The next day, another, and the next another. Finally, she opened up. Without realizing it, he had reached her in the way that mattered most to her: She was an intensely spiritual woman, but in the midst of her tragedy, she had been having a crisis of faith. This was the one key that would open her door.

Upon her discharge from the hospital, my associate referred her to me for treatment. Though she was full of mistrust and still reluctant to talk to anyone, I let her know by my silent acceptance that it was safe to bring out her feelings in her own time. Slowly, a connection was made. She began to tell her story.

She had been a happy child, with loving parents and a warm household. When she was 7 years old, her mother became very ill and was taken away to the hospital. One day shortly before Christmas, her father took her out of school. She was full of excitement thinking how special she was that her father came, in front of all the other children, to take her somewhere "important." In fact, they were headed to the hospital to see her mother for the last time.

Jennifer, not knowing the real reason for the visit, thought they were taking her mother home and that all would be right again. When her mother was wheeled toward her in a wheelchair, Jennifer was shocked at how "different" she looked. But they were going to take her home and all would be well.

Jennifer was devastated when she was told to say goodbye and that her mother would not be going with them. She described to me in vivid detail, as if reliving it all over again, her feelings at that moment: "All I wanted was to go with her, be with her, stay with her forever." She never saw her mother again.

Her father remarried shortly after her mother's death and forbade the children to talk of their mother. This completed Jennifer's sense of betrayal and abandonment. Now she had lost both parents. She was forced to call her stepmother "Mom" and did so only with the hope of pleasing her father and winning back his love. It didn't work. She began living a life of outward compliance, while inwardly she was building a fantasy world where she could stay close to her mother. She imagined that her mother would come back from the grave, and her happiness would be restored as it once was.

She made her accommodations to life and grew older. Emotionally estranged from her father and stepmother, she looked forward to the chance to get out on her own. When it was time, she found a college "as far away from home as possible." Despite great discouragement and against tremendous odds, she went to college and financed her own way through. There she found many friends, a new life, and a couple of surrogate "parents" with whom she lived.

I believe she would have made a successful adaptation to life if she had not gone back home after college. This was the trap that finally ensnared her in the tragedy that was to follow.

Upon moving back home, she found her father and step-mother to be just as unreceptive as before. She set about busily creating her own life. Working three jobs at the same time, she had her sights set on buying a first house. She worked long hours, rushing from one job to another, building toward her dream. Finally, she had enough for the down payment and a mortgage.

She moved into her new home, and just a few days later, while hanging wallpaper, she felt a sharp pain in her back. She could not afford to admit that it might be serious. As she continued working and fixing up her house, her back condition worsened. Despite her resistance, she told her father and stepmother about it. They gave her an implicit message of disapproval and told her to ignore it. Finally, one day, she collapsed on the floor.

This was the beginning of eleven surgeries and the loss of most feeling from her waist down. She would be paralyzed for the rest of her life.

These several months later, as I heard her story in my office, the picture came together in my mind. She had been finding fulfillment by escaping her disappointment in her family. But upon her return, she fell prey to the old dynamics once again. She still wanted her father's love, to at least reclaim that much of her childhood happiness. When her back problem first developed, she had secret hopes that he would at last come back to her in a gesture of love and caring. But she was caught; her father had given her the message, she should not cry or complain. She had to be a "good" girl. And so she continued working through the increasingly severe pain until she fell to the floor and could not get up.

Perhaps, too, she was unconsciously reaching for her mother by trying to become like her. Now she, too, was in a wheelchair. She, too, had been in the hospital. She, too, would leave the world, if not physically, then through emotional withdrawal, to be with her mother. She had re-created the last moments of her innocence, the episode in the hospital when she still had both parents who loved her.

It was at this time that the depths of her fantasy world revealed themselves, as she started expressing to me her literal expectation that her mother would come back. Only through the strength of our therapeutic alliance—something much more than professionalism, something more of a sharing of souls on the journey together—could she reveal such a thing and, in revealing it, expose it for the fantasy it was.

Slowly, very slowly, she started opening up to life again. Making peace with her stepmother, accepting the limitations of her father, she began investing her energies not in trying to retrieve the past and bring it back to life, but in receiving the life that was waiting to be lived all around her. She knew my commitment to her, and she held on to the hope that the fulfillment I told her was waiting for her was possible. She made the choice to live again.

She began expressing her Joy by pouring out her love—significantly, her motherly love—onto her two nieces. This was the opportunity to be accepted by people who needed her and whom she could need. If she could not have the love of her mother, and was unable to have children of her own, she would fill this void by giving her love to her nieces. Sublimating her old pain in new and life-affirming ways, she invested herself fully into these girls and found comfort and fulfillment.

Shortly after this time, she was in danger of losing her job, which had been held for her through her illness. If she lost her job, she would lose her house and that meant everything to her. The desire to keep her house became another point of interest to help her set her sights on living in the world again. But for three days, when setting out to go back to work, this time in a wheelchair, she found herself unconsciously turning from the back door to the basement door. She spent three days hiding in the basement, retreating into her fantasy world. On the fourth day I saw her and gave her comfort. Reminding her of her strength by surrounding her with my own, she made it to work the next day. She would keep her house. Her reentry into the world had begun!

Through the next months, as she went through a demanding training program and succeeded, her strengths built. At first alienated from her coworkers, she began slowly making contacts. Around this time, she expressed a wish for a dog. Immediately, she would discourage herself with the thought "I can't walk a dog." My associate, the psychiatrist who first visited her in the hospital, heard of this and suggested she get a long leash and hold it from the back door. Today, she loves and is loved by a beautiful cocker spaniel.

Not long after, she bought a car with hand gears. She was mobile again. This opened up the possibility of travel. Her first trip was back to her college to visit her beloved "family" there. She was welcomed as if she had never left. Other trips took her cross country and up and down the East Coast several times. Developing an avid interest in the wilderness, she has gone on several camping weekends, taking her dog and nieces with her, and has fallen in love with the Appalachian mountains.

Jennifer recently celebrated her fortieth birthday at a surprise party thrown by her friends and coworkers. If "a tree is known by its fruit," the evidences of the sweetness of this tree are everywhere. It has been one of my great privileges to know this woman and to participate in her journey back into life, a life she is living to the full, free from the fears of the past.

This journey to wholeness is possible for us all. The necessary tools are available, and no one need feel their particular circumstances exempt them from it. For the meaning and power of such circumstances come only from our interpretation of them. Facing the fear shows the interpretation to be false, as the imagined consequences do not affect us as we believed they would. The seemingly impenetrable wall that blocked our way becomes a holographic illusion as we walk straight through it into Joy.

And so, Joy and fear are cast as the main players in our human drama, our journey back Home. Joy is the "stuff" of consciousness, the soul-essence of who we are and what our universe is. Fear is a distorting filter, imposing a cast of joylessness on all that we see. The key to happiness, the way to radical Joy, is to find and face this "illusion" of fear, and watch it dissolve as the mirage it always was.

This is the great quest of our lives. We can either delay the time when we embark upon it, causing ourselves needless suffering, or we can choose it *now* and begin to truly live.

# EXERCISES

## Exercise 1: Listing Your Fears

Begin the process of finding fear simply by writing down the series of fears, mundane and sublime, which stop you from living a life of Joy. Buy a special notebook for this purpose, to be used in many of the exercises which follow. This will become your "Workbook for Radical Joy."

When making your list, it is important to remember that fear comes in many colors. Anything which is not ultimately about Joy has fear at its root. It could be something that makes you angry, sad, guilty, embarrassed, jealous, ashamed, or bored. Each of these, and all other negative states, are really fear in disguise.

Look at those things which cause you unrest throughout your day. Look at responses you have to your immediate and global surroundings. Look at your longings, your unfulfilled dreams. In each of these situations, some hidden fear has kept you from acting in the way that Joy would prescribe.

Imagine, too, how you would feel if the circumstances of your life were to change or disappear—if money, health, family, freedom, or any of the "givens" you may take for granted were suddenly taken away from you.

You may have to look beneath the surface of a particular problem to find the fear that is driving it. If, for example, money seems to be the reason you can't fulfill your dreams, look at the obstacles *underneath* this obstacle, such as the fear of doing what it takes to make more money. So, too, with changing your living circumstances, having more time, or even having better health. Ask yourself, "What is the fear that keeps me from doing that which would correct these situations?"

Finally, look at what stops you from being the kind of person you want to be—mentally, physically, and spiritually—and think especially about the contribution you want to make with your life, to see the world of your highest Vision realized. What fears stop you from taking the first step toward this vision? Make the list as long as you want; the longer the better. Carry a pad and pen with you and add to your list as you go along.

Remember, your list should include items that may not appear to be fearful at all. Perhaps they will look like boredom, annoyance or embarrassment. But anything which does not promote Joy does hide some form of fear. Use this exercise to practice getting familiar with the many varieties of fear that come along throughout your day.

Let's take this exercise very seriously. As the Zen saying goes, we should come to this "as if our hair were on fire." Life is intense! And it will not do any longer to continue with the illusion of ordinariness. We want to get caught up in the possibility of extraordinary living. We want to release ourselves from *all* fear (yes, this is possible), to realize the Joy that can come only with freedom from arbitrary limits. Let's bring the fullness of our passion for Joy to these exercises, that we may find and face our fears, watching them dissolve as the mirage they always were.

## FEARS—Sample List

1. Standing up to my boss
2. Changing my job
3. Job interviews
4. Taking a financial risk
5. Working too hard and not getting enough sleep
6. Not having enough money and becoming homeless
7. Loneliness
8. Dating
9. Obligatory social events
10. Dieting
11. Being late
12. Dying
13. Never fulfilling my dreams

## Exercise 2: Cost-Benefit Analysis

Next, in your Workbook, list the costs and apparent benefits of fear. Of course, we choose our fears for a reason—they seem to offer some benefit. If we really examine what this benefit is, we can begin to expose the illusion it is hiding, and understand its cost without needing to defend our choice. This is an essential step in being willing to face the imagined threat of fear so that we may let it go completely.

All fear seems to offer safety of some sort—if we are afraid, we will stay vigilant to the signs that warn of impending attack. And of course, all fear exacts a cost. It costs us our peace and sense of well-being. Living under fear, we are caught in a chronic state of "fight or flight," always protecting and defending, ever anticipating future threat, never free to enjoy where we are here and now. The ultimate cost of fear is in the way it keeps us from really living, from taking those actions which would allow us to be fulfilled, expressed, and self-actualized.

To begin this exercise, choose several of the fears from the list you made in Exercise 1. Next to each, write out the benefits you have believed it held for you. Put these on the left side of a page. On the right side, list the costs of the fear. Again, the point of this exercise is simply to raise awareness. We are only at the beginning stages of our work, and awareness is the first step.

As you go through this process, ask yourself the following questions:

- Is the benefit of holding this fear something I truly enjoy, or does it merely offer safety from a problem?
- How much tension is involved in protecting against potential problems this way?
- How much am I willing to risk this "security" to truly live and enjoy life?

- Would it be exciting to take such a risk, daring to let life take me on an adventure?
- What would be possible (something I've always wanted but thought was impossible) if I did so?

### *Sample List*

## Fear 1: Standing Up To My Boss

| Benefits | Costs |
| --- | --- |
| I have a good excuse for not advancing my career. I can blame my boss for my poor performance at work. Others will have sympathy and not expect as much from me. | I don't get to make things happen when I use these excuses. I carry around a constant resentment toward my boss. This rules my mind and saps my energy and Joy. |

## Fear 2: Dieting

| Benefits | Costs |
| --- | --- |
| Others won't blame me for being overweight if they know I'm afraid to diet. I don't have to deal with being disapproved of for my looks; I can blame it on my weight. Eating is nurturing to me. | My health and vitality suffer when I'm overweight. I feel victimized by my weight problem, as if I don't have control over my life. I lose important opportunities for meeting people. |

## Fear 3: Dating

| Benefits | Costs |
| --- | --- |
| I never have to face the fear of rejection if I don't go on dates. I have a good excuse to stay close to my family and not leave home. | I stay lonely and isolated. My life is passing by and I'm not creating my dream of marriage and a family of my own. I have to sacrifice what I want, to live in my parents' world. |

## Exercise 3: Choosing Three Fears to Face

Now we are ready to take our first tentative steps toward Joy. Pick three of the fears on your list from Exercise 1 and make the commitment to face them. Do what the fear would prevent you from doing, while anticipating your release into freedom—freedom from the belief that you are powerless over your fear, freedom from the belief that something terrible will happen if you face this fear. Walk straight through the illusion of threat to find your Joy welcoming you with open arms on the other side.

But it is important to be wise in taking this first step. You don't want to face something that is too threatening too quickly, or that might discourage you from taking further steps. Find three fears that you are *ready* to take on. Choose your actions according to what would give you a feeling of release, freedom, and excitement as well as an incipient sense of power over your fears. Choose those fears you feel confident you can banish, even though you may be afraid at the same time. Again, you don't want to end up running away before getting through to the other side.

This is not an exercise in denial; it is not about ignoring the consequences. We have to expose fear in order to face it, and cannot afford to pretend we are unafraid. Be aware of the fear that may impel you to plunge blindly in. Facing your fear, you may find that you are not ready to take all the actions you set out to take. Be sure to respect the wisdom of your present level of readiness.

Nevertheless, we do want to bring the full intensity of our commitment to this practice, for we have been living for too many years with too much pain and too little fulfillment. Find the fear that has been keeping you there!

Our old strategy of "safety through fear" hurts. If we have, for example, been devoting ourselves to making money, originally to have the means to find Joy, we must ask ourselves, are we *getting* to that Joy? There is the very real possibility that we are simply following a routine, never getting free of our misery, and thinking ultimately that that is all there is to expect from life. This is choosing to be "right" rather than "happy," choosing security over Joy. Let us instead feel the thrill of not knowing where our "security" is coming from, but being free to live fully. And as we face this fear, we discover the true security of Joy. Would we not prefer to live fully than to have all the security in the world and be caught in a meaningless routine from which there was never any relief? As a friend of mine once said, "I prefer to lose a leg and be happy than to have both my legs and be unhappy." This is choosing for Joy! For in the end, *it does not matter what we do, who we are, or what we have in life. It only matters that we are happy doing, having, and being these things!*

There is a cartoon of a man in hell, pushing his wheelbarrow full of coals, whistling happily as he does so. One devil pops up from behind a rock and says to another devil, "He doesn't seem to be getting the idea!" In fact, this is the picture of someone who has realized himself. Our circumstances don't have the power to determine our happiness; happiness is a choice. And when we get wise to the costs and benefits of our choices and find the motivation to face our fears, we can create our happiness wherever we are.

As you follow this exercise, name each fear, then write down, in sequence, the experience you have in facing that fear (1) before, (2) during, and (3) after. Note who you are in the presence of your fear—what thoughts and feelings you have— and how your relationship to the fear changes as you move through. Follow this pattern for each fear you practice with, so that you can refer back to your notebook when the fear is strong, and be encouraged.

## *Choosing Three Fears to Face—Sample*
### Fear 1: Standing Up To My Boss

Before:

> Anticipating rejection, fantasizing about the scenario in my mind and a terrible outcome: my boss yelling at me, belittling me in front of my coworkers, coworkers laughing at me. Sweaty palms, racing heart. Keep trying to put my mind on other things but not able to. I remind myself why I'm doing this: It's worse not to go through with it.

During:

> My heart is racing like crazy, but I'm more focused on saying the right thing, controlling my voice, reading my boss's face and body language. It's like an altered state, time sort of stands still, as I become so absorbed in what's happening in the moment. I'm almost detached, just calmly observing, just watching myself and the situation.

After:

> Exhilaration, the contrast between the tension I felt and this relief! My boss said he'll think about it—he didn't laugh at all! I realize how much I was making things overly dramatic in my mind. It's really no big deal. Most of what we think about is really no big deal. And it's fun and a little bit exciting to face my fears.

# CHAPTER 2

# THE CREATION STORY REVISITED

The knowledge of the ancients was perfect. How perfect?
At first, they did not know that there were things.
This is the most perfect knowledge; nothing can be
added. Next, they knew there were things, but did
not yet make distinctions between them. Next, they made
distinctions between them, but they did not yet pass
judgments upon them. When judgments were passed,
the Way was destroyed.

—Chuang-tzu

How did we come to be in this state of affairs? What had us choose fear in the first place if it is only an illusion? A visit to the creation story, with new perspective, holds the clues to our answer.

## Oneness and Separation

All the great creation myths tell of our original perfection. In this perfection, there was no place that Joy was absent. All was a Oneness, with no differences to cause any separation from Joy. We were part of this perfection and still carry the memory of it deeply within.

Suddenly there appeared a rift, a separation, a rent in the Oneness. With this, the world of opposites was born. Joy would now be known by its contrast to fear, and Oneness by its contrast to separation.

The crucial twist in the story, the critical insight given here, comes when we realize that we *chose* this separation, wishing it into existence. Some teachings have described this as a "tiny mad idea," others as a playful challenge. Whatever the interpretation, we went forth upon a quest for an experience "other" than the perfection of Oneness. Somehow, we believed, this would give us "more" than what we knew.

But how could we accomplish this feat? If the Oneness was all-encompassing, there could be nothing more to find and nowhere else to look for it. Our solution to this dilemma was to "fall asleep," like Adam in the Garden, and dream the dream that it was so. Adam falls asleep and Eve is created as his "other." They then eat of the tree of the knowledge of Good and Evil, of duality, and in so doing, their innocence is lost. They cover their "nakedness" with shame and are cast out of the Garden of Oneness.

This is the dream we are still dreaming, a dream that would show us the pictures and give us the experiences we wished for. If we wanted to know that which was other than the perfect Joy of Oneness, we would dream of a "place" that was separate from It. This was the beginning of the world, as we projected ourselves "outside" the Oneness that was everywhere and into the dream of our making.

## How to Build a World

In dreaming up a place that was the opposite of Oneness, we would design it to be a place where fear, not Joy, ruled. We would design a place where the forces of separation would divide the Oneness into discrete parts or "things," and then locate these things in separate places and times. "Now" would be separated from "then"; "here" would be separated from "there."

We would fragment the one Mind into many minds and surround each with a body, a fenced-off area to distinguish one from the other. These, too, would be situated at discrete points of time and space, that we could begin to give them identity and distinction. Everything would then be divided into that which is "inside" the body and that which is "outside" it. In this way, the body would become the ultimate separator between "me" and the rest of the world.

These bodies would further differentiate what is "before" us and what is "behind" us, what is "above" us and what is "underneath" us, as we designed them with a front and a back, a top and a bottom. Such orientation would give points of reference by which to establish the configuration of space.

Gravity, too, created by the "attraction" of bodies, would work in concert with space and time to create such orientation, that "up" and "down" and "closer" and "farther" may describe basic markers for ordering our new world. And such bodies would have "senses," ways of registering these markers of space and time, to confirm that indeed these things "exist" outside the body.

But these reference-making, organizing devices are our own creation! We dreamt them up to convince ourselves that the separation was real, when all the while we remain in the perfect union of Oneness. And the body's senses, which seem to give solid evidence for the "objective" reality of it all, are but further ruses for our scheme. We see and hear only what we have predetermined to see and hear. For if we were to register accurately what is "going on out there," we would see but the same Oneness everywhere, with no distinction between "inside of us" and "outside," "self" or "other," "sacred" and "profane."

Nevertheless, we continued to dream the dream. If the body's senses show us the independent existence of things-out-there, then we must be standing apart from these things, observing from a different place. This sets up the great and final subterfuge of Oneness, the ultimate plot for perpetuating the separation: If we are separate from the rest of what is "out there," we are vulnerable to the experience of lack— the experience of missing the things that we "need." We must then begin to seek "outside" ourselves to find our missing parts, lest external forces threaten to leave us forever unwhole and wanting. We must reintegrate the other "fragments" of ourselves, knowing that originally we were/are one with them and they with us, so that we may restore ourselves to our true state.

With this we embarked on the human journey, the search for happiness, believing that we had lost our original innocence and must find it "somewhere out there" to be whole again. Such a search is driven by the dictates of separation. It is fueled by the idea that our Joy has been confiscated and is being hidden in some faraway cave, protected by mists of obscurity, fire-breathing dragons or other perils. To win back our birthright, we must begin an arduous journey fraught with dangers, as we move through the great distance which separates us from Joy.

Once we see ourselves as tiny, isolated fragments of Mind, trapped within bodies, we must look for the many fragments out there that would restore our wholeness. Rather than recognize the fact that we dreamt up this entire idea, we would preserve it by busily engaging in the search outside ourselves for a joy that has been lost, thereby confirming that we must indeed be lacking within. We launch upon the journey of forever looking for our "missing parts," knowing secretly that we will never succeed for we are looking in the wrong direction.

We can feel the compelling nature of our search; each time we set a new goal, dream of a better future, or long for the resurrection of the past, we are prompted to exercise our own efforts, obsessed with finding the way to make it happen. We search for the ideal lover, the overthrown government, the new car, the perfect children, or the house with the white picket fence, believing these things will bring us the Joy we seek. The piece of chocolate cake or the bottle of alcohol promises salvation if only we can hold and possess it. Even religion is used for this purpose; the greatest oxymoron ever invented is the "holy war," the attempt to "win" some prized missing part for the supposed glory of God.

And so, the entire world of our human experience is but an illusion we are playing out. For behind the scenes, we are wholly responsible for the set and design of this great theatrical production, having created its existence and our response to it. The attempted moral of the play is that separation, not Oneness, is the rule. Indeed, every object, every situation, and even every idea of our world speaks to independent identity, bearing witness to the "reality" of separation, the nonexistence of Oneness.

## Buying into Fear

And now for the development of fear. As we continued to dream of a world "apart," we began building a more and more elaborate defense against the memory of Oneness. In imagining an experience different from our original innocence, we would create the idea that we were "guilty" for having separated. We would decide that we had "sinned" and were to be judged accordingly. This, we dreamed, was cause for fear, as we anticipated certain retaliation for our terrible deed. Again, in the Eden metaphor, when Adam and Eve ate of the tree of the knowledge of good and evil, their innocence was lost; they covered their "nakedness" with shame. Never having conceived of self and other, they became *self*-conscious, worried about how they were to be regarded by God. When God visited them, they tried to hide themselves before being cast out into the world of separation.

And so fear became our constant companion. Fear that we were separate from our wholeness, that what we needed could be taken from us. Fear that others would attack us because they were experiencing the same deprivation. Time and space not only became the great separators, but the great agents of fear as well; indeed, they are created as the sequential layout of fear, the patterning devices that would separate us from our Good. Our Joy was to become something of the past or yet to come; it would be found in something "over there" or "far away" but never "here." And the curriculum for finding Joy again would now require that we work our way through events and experiences that must be "lived through," each such event or experience marking the coordinates of the space-time continuum. With this, we begin our seeking—seeking but never finding. And the Oneness goes on uninterrupted all the while.

To confront our guilt, to take responsibility for it, was not an option. Doing so would force us to recognize that we had fabricated the whole thing. Our solution, instead, would be to project the guilt outward—onto other people or the Creator, and believe that it was they who had done something wrong. This, we hoped, would relieve our guilt while protecting us from the awareness of our "sin" and the fear of retribution.

We built an entire world from this projection, a world in which we could hide from or repress the awareness that we had dreamt it all up. And so, projection and repression, twin offspring of fear, became favorite tools for keeping the truth out of reach. We became so skilled at these that we (almost) completely forgot there could be anything else. The dream became "reality."

## Living the Separation

These were the first moments of separation. The story of our suffering, then, is clear: The fragments of mind, the "skin-encapsulated egos," housed within a body, would seek for Joy according to the prescriptions of fear, always looking *outside ourselves* for our "missing parts," believing that finding them would bring us the Joy we seek. Thus was born the ego, the individual self, the human mind. Its purpose is to keep us from waking up from the dream, from remembering that the secret to Joy is within, that the idea of fear is something we have chosen. This is the human condition in which we find ourselves today. This is the very source of all that we experience.

The real value in all this is that we may understand we are reinventing the separation moment-to-moment, with each thought we think, with each choice for fear! We are, even now, recreating the separation, keeping out the memory of Oneness (which goes on uninterrupted while we dream) each time we look outside ourselves. Suddenly, the unconscious plotting of our everyday mind is illuminated in all its nakedness. We are still trying to convince ourselves that we are not the naturally joyful beings we were created to be. And the reasons we do all that we do now become blatantly clear as well: We are attempting to find our Joy, distracting ourselves with external stimulation, while avoiding the inner journey to where Joy actually lives. Fear becomes an effective tool to convince us not to look within, to disguise the Truth from us. With this realization, it is harder to continue denying Joy, easier to undo our mistakes by facing the fear of looking within. Instead of continuing on the path of unfulfillment, trying to prove ourselves unworthy of Joy, let us discover the true humility that comes with accepting reality and the Joy it naturally bestows upon us.

For freedom from this messy state of affairs comes with the awakening realization that we have not, in truth, ever separated. Whether by a surrender forced upon us from too many years of pain, or a faithful trust that there is more to life than what the world would have us believe, we give up the game and allow reality to penetrate our illusions. When it does, we spontaneously realize the secret to Joy: *We are already whole and complete, perfect and innocent, just the way we are.* We do not need to change anything about ourselves or the world, and do not need to seek anywhere else for fulfillment. Our mission to find our missing parts "out there," that which we believe would make us happy and restore our original wholeness, now becomes a matter of transforming our fear into Joy by recognizing the perfection of things *as they are*. For in the Oneness, there is no need, no lack, but only the experience of ongoing Fulfillment, ever-present and all-complete.

And with this also comes the realization that there is nothing—and never *was* anything—to fear. If the separation has never occurred and we have, in fact, never "sinned," then there is no reason to be punished. And no reason to search for missing parts to bolster ourselves and make ourselves more powerful, more powerful than each other and more powerful than the God who, we believe, wants to attack us—both the victims of our projected guilt.

This means that everything we experience in the world is a misunderstanding of what is perfectly in accord with the Oneness . . . still. All that is needful, then, in our quest for Joy is to recognize and accept this fact. If our fear is purely the result of our dreamlike imaginings, we have good reason to face the fear of looking within, letting go of the distractions of external seeking.

Once again, the only thing that makes this difficult is our continuing choice to stay separate from Oneness and original Joy. We still believe that we can make life "work better" by trying to arrange circumstances to our liking. These are our dreams, plans, and defenses for the life we believe will get us what we want. We insist that our way must be right, and if we will only try one more time, we will succeed. Instead of continuing on this loveless path, let us give up the dream so that reality may show us its benevolent nature, and we may take our rightful place in a friendly universe.

With true understanding, the fear and separation experiences of our lives can become the vehicles by which we rediscover our Joy. In facing our fears and recognizing them for what they are, this Joy extends in an ever-widening circle. For Joy is infectious, and others are swept up in its possibility by our example. In setting ourselves free, we demonstrate that the fears that would keep us separate are so much empty stuff, and nothing has the power to disturb our Peace.

This is the final Homecoming, wherein the world is healed, and Joy comes to earth at last.

# EXERCISES

## Exercise 1: The Separation in Everyday Life

If we recreate the separation with each "fear thought," then our task in finding Joy can be described as the "undoing" of all this. As always, however, it is first necessary to develop awareness of the problem—awareness of how we are, in fact, recreating the separation. Specifically, we want to practice being aware of when and why we are judging, for our judgments are ways of saying that something about the world is wrong and should be changed. This is the moment of separation, where we separate ourselves from reality-as-it-is, keeping ourselves from the awareness of why things are the way they are, and the Joy such awareness holds for us.

Our practice in this exercise involves catching ourselves in the act of judging and finding the fear that has us doing so, seeing how it separates us from the rest of the world. With this, we pave the way to recognizing that everything is already just as it should be.

In your Workbook:

- Write in the left-hand column those judgments you catch yourself in the act of making, as soon as you are able to stop and write them down.
- In the middle column, write down the fear from your list in Chapter 1 (or a new fear if you discover one not on the list) that underlies this judgment.
- In the right-hand column, write down the cost and benefit of holding this judgment.

The *cost* of your judgment will involve something that separates you from your Good, from others you are judging, from a connection with your environment, and so forth.

As for the *benefit* of our judgments, we believe that judging will give us some reward, usually in the form of protection. Perhaps we will feel safe from inferiority if we judge another negatively. Perhaps we will keep ourselves from having to take responsibility for effecting change if we judge ourselves unworthy or "less than" another.

Of course, all of these are false benefits compared to the potential for Joy that comes with releasing judgment and freeing ourselves from fear. But for this exercise, it is important not to be too concerned with letting go of our judgments. Without the strengthening of our character, we may compound the problem if we try to let go of our judgments too soon: We don't want to judge ourselves as guilty for having judgments! So let your attitude at this point be one of relaxed attention, not straining too much to "fix" yourself but simply devoting yourself to training your awareness. If you are able, in a flowing and joyous way, to let go of your judgments as you become aware of them, so be it. Otherwise, be assured that this is very much our goal for future exercises.

### Sample

| Judgment | Fear Underneath This Judgment | Cost | Benefit |
|---|---|---|---|
| 1. My boss doesn't care about what his employees think; I can't make a difference here. | I fear my boss's disapproval if I suggest a change and he doesn't like it. | I don't get the chance to make a difference, to get my work life to be more meaningful. | I don't have to assume responsibility for the way things are. |

| Judgment | Fear Underneath This Judgment | Cost | Benefit |
|---|---|---|---|
| 2. Amy is a better athlete than I am; I can't compete against her. | I'll look foolish if I compete against her and lose. | I deprive myself of the chance to do what I love, win or lose. I can't improve my performance without testing my limits. | I get to keep the image of being successful if I don't compete; I avoid rejection and keep the praise. |

## Exercise 2: The Separation in Our Life Choices

In this exercise, we go through the same process as above, this time looking at the life choices we have made and the ways they have taken us into separation. All of us started out with a relatively pure experience of Oneness; not having devised the fears and defenses which would build our later personality, we knew ourselves to be connected with everything around us. But we came to experience separation, and as our life circumstances met us, we found our way to fear.

Let us now examine the ways that we have chosen fear in some of the life choices we have made, and again, break it down into the same three columns we used in Exercise 1. This will begin to flesh out the life journey we have taken, from Oneness to separation, a process we will pursue further in the next chapter.

- Pick three or more such life choices and look for the judgment in each of them.

  Be aware that any guilt, unworthiness, or powerlessness

you may have thought was the reason for your choice, is still the judgment that says "things should not be the way they are." We made our choice in direct response to this, trying to change "the way things were," thereby declaring ourselves separate from "what was."

- For each choice, fill in the same three columns as before—Judgment; Fear that Underlies this Judgment; Cost/Benefit.

As you go through this exercise, you may begin to see certain patterns emerge which shed light on fundamental aspects of who you are. These are the patterns that make up our personality, the subject of our next chapter.

### Sample

## Life Choice 1: Not Going to College

| Judgment | Fear Underneath This Judgment | Cost | Benefit |
|---|---|---|---|
| I'm not smart enough; it would be too much work to get through; what you learn isn't about real life or what's important. | I'll risk failing. I'll have to do things I don't enjoy. I'll lose my freedom to do what I want and get locked into the rat race. | I'll close many doors by not going to college. I'll miss the opportunity to grow and learn. I'll miss the opportunity to rise above my fear. | I get to do what I want and stay a "free spirit" a little longer. I can take it easy for now and postpone the question of what to do with my life. |

## Life Choice 2: Taking the Job I Didn't Love

| Judgment | Fear Underneath This Judgment | Cost | Benefit |
|---|---|---|---|
| I'm not capable of getting the job I really want. It's a jungle out there; too much competition. | Others will think I'm foolish for not taking this job. I'm afraid of not having the security of this job if I go for what I really want. | I'll sacrifice my passion and chance to make my life meaningful for the sake of "security." I won't get to discover who I really am and my life's purpose. | I get to be more comfortable with the idea of not going hungry, being able to pay my bills, etc. I get approval from others for this. |

# CHAPTER 3

# THE MAKING OF A PERSONALITY

Only a little wall of dust still stands between you [and Joy]. Blow on it lightly and with happy laughter, and it will fall away.

—*A Course in Miracles*

We have been exploring the early stages of our work, understanding that in order to find Joy we must first find and face our fear. And to do this, we must be curious about our fear—study it, shake hands with it, and come to peace with it. Like putting clothes on the invisible man, the fear takes shape and we recognize it for what it truly is.

It is not difficult to find our fears; they are not actually invisible. The problem is that, while we have imagined them to be too intolerable even to look at, we have tightly shut our eyes, flailing about wildly in defense against some unseen threat. We convince ourselves that it must be threatening indeed, else we would not be behaving so fearfully. But all of this is done in imagination. Someone once said, "My life was full of terrible misfortunes ... most of which never happened." Only while we keep our eyes shut can we continue to believe such fantasies and respond to them as if they were real.

In this chapter we will take a major step forward toward Joy, opening our eyes and looking fear boldly in the face. Tracing it back to its source at the birth of our personality, we will see how it is living on in the present, distorting our perception, controlling and shaping our lives. This and only this holds the key to Freedom and Fulfillment.

## The Core Fear and Chief Defense

Each of us is born in Joy. Watch any newborn and the feeling is unmistakable. But then something happens—a trauma, an abandonment, a loss of love. Suddenly, we are thrust into a new experience: fear. The threatening situation is registered in consciousness as something to be constantly on the alert about. It becomes what we will call the "core fear." We are ever-watchful for the signs that warn of it happening again.

We seek out a strategy for dealing with this fear, something that will ensure protection against the threat. This strategy will become our "chief defense." It is the blueprint for how we will respond to fear in future situations. Some of us become extra "good" or "careful," assuming that the problem was the result of something we did. Others decide that someone else is at fault, and they become angry and demanding. Still others become withdrawn, depressed, or helpless, waiting to be rescued. This is the critical choice that sets our life course, and gives birth to the wide variety of human behavior.

From the moment of original threat, we use the core fear as a "watchdog" to alert us to the possibility of further threat. And we use the chief defense to do everything in our power to keep it from ever happening again. Our entire being orients itself toward protection in this way, so that we may preserve the integrity of who we are. There is an enemy in our midst and we must build the fortress walls around our Joy securely.

The core fear and chief defense become a response style. We will interpret every situation through the lens of this dynamic duo. Promising never to experience such a threat again, the core fear has us see the signs of threat everywhere, while the chief defense prepares to either admit the experience or fend it off with its favorite maneuver.

These events are the seeds of personality. When first we find our solution for dealing with crisis, we feel a vast relief and resolve to keep responding that way. We have found our strategy for living, a way of relating to the world that gives us power and makes life turn out the way we want. This creates a tremendous addictive pull, and knowing little else, we feel that we have discovered the secret to getting our needs met. We will do it again and again and again.

All of our upsets boil down to the core fear. It is the distilled essence of our anxieties, angers, jealousies, and guilts. Our core fear may be initiated by a single traumatic event, a series of subtler influences, or simply a pervading atmosphere of threat. But once we land upon this interpretation of life, it becomes the thought cluster, the template, upon which we define all future experience.

Similarly, each of our defenses has, as its root, the chief defense. "People pleasers," for example, may adopt a posture of submissiveness, never expressing their own needs, sacrificing themselves for others. Alternatively, they may choose the role of "the good provider," "the dutiful wife," "the cute little boy," or "the clown," all by way of attempting to please others and avoid the core fear of abandonment.

As we move through life, fear compounds with fear. Again if we are afraid of abandonment, we may be worried at one moment about being criticized, thinking we will not be loved if found to be imperfect. In the next moment, we can fret about financial security, as if money were our ticket to acceptance. A new moment may have us holding on to the past when we felt loved, afraid of the possibility of rejection in the present.

These are the interactions of the core fear with the variety of life's circumstances.

Our defenses can build on top of each other as well. The people pleaser might well find herself becoming angry or judgmental in secret, where it is safe to let off steam as long as no one knows about it. The structure of our defense can take on incredible complexity and sophistication. We may believe, for instance, that by standing up for ourselves, breaking free of the habit of people pleasing, we will be approved of by others who are coaching us in this direction. Despite appearances, it is still the chief defense, the search for approval, that is motivating our actions.

The core fear spawns all of our interpretations of life, and the chief defense spawns all of our behaviors. It doesn't matter how complex we get; all we need to know is that each of our problems boils down to the core fear and chief defense. Whenever we are not wholly joyous, we can be sure these two are hard at work at the source of our trouble. As we dance the dance of life, we use our chief defense to skillfully navigate through the pitfalls of the core fear, in the attempt to recapture our original Joy.

This is the history of the world. With each new human birth and the development of a personality, we repeat the same story, believing that to keep a constant watch for fear is to make ourselves safe and thereby protect our Joy. Let's look now at some personal stories that highlight the ways in which the core fear and chief defense shape our experience and set the course of our lives.

## Julie

Julie, a 47-year-old woman, came for therapy because she was unhappy in her marriage. She wanted more out of life than "being a housewife and baking cookies." She was 130 pounds overweight and, while attractive, did not present herself as such. Going back to the source of her core fear, she discovered the place where her life strategy had begun. At eight years old, she had been repeatedly molested by her father. Seeking comfort and protection from her mother, she was instead given the message that if she dared tell anyone, her father would be sent away and the family would fall apart.

Hopelessly conflicted over this betrayal by parents whom she had loved and trusted, Julie found her chief defense: She would bury all needs. She became, in her own words, a "frozen rabbit," always quiet and unassuming, ever-attentive to the needs of others, afraid of making a wrong move. Further, she began eating excessively to "stuff" her own needs and used the extra weight as protection, making herself unattractive to her father.

As she grew older, she became extremely self-sufficient, not needing anything from anybody, taking on the role instead of providing for others. She found a husband who related to her as a child to a mother, allowing her to take full charge of the household. Throughout life, she would fortify her defenses in this way, taking the attention off her own needs and solving problems by attending to the needs of others.

In her therapy, it was pointed out that her self-sufficiency, while a talent to be used when helpful, was a compulsion over which she had no control. Her belief that she didn't "need" anything was itself an overpowering need. She *needed* to not need anything. In fact, this need was running her life. She had no freedom to choose her course; the need was making decisions for her. It was the reason for her coming to therapy, the source of her unfulfillment. At that moment, she realized she had been living out this scenario her entire life, burying her needs in all of her relationships—with parents, with friends, and especially in her marriage.

Against great anxiety, she took up my invitation to begin expressing her needs in the therapy. Soon, she became like a little child, feeling again the terrible insecurity of the eight-year-old girl whose parents had abandoned and betrayed her.

Seizing the opportunity, I asked her what I could do for her, how I could meet her need in that moment. When she replied, "I need to tell you what he [my father] did, and I need you to believe me," a huge flood of tears burst forth from behind the dam of a lifetime of repression, and she poured out all the pain that had been buried, emotionally and under her excess weight, through the years. Finally, she was quiet. A soft glow of peace came over her, and the face of the eight-year-old little girl began to transform before my eyes into that of a mature woman with a quiet confidence and a solid sense of self.

Since that time, she has shed over 100 pounds and changed her hairstyle for a much more attractive appearance. She has also taken the name she was called as a child—Julia—preferring it to Julie, but too afraid until now to associate with it. Her marriage, once the source of her greatest pain, has become a powerful vehicle for her self-discovery and growth. She has opened up sexually to her husband, expressing her needs to him and healing much of the pain from the past. She has gone on to get her credentials as an Interfaith minister and conducts beautiful liturgy services for a growing audience. In her own words, "I feel as though my life now holds endless possibilities."

## Susan

Susan, a 44-year-old mother and part-time librarian, had a similar story, demonstrating how the core fear and chief defense set our personality structures, determine our response styles, and dictate our strategies for living.

She originally came to see me for depression and low self-esteem, both of which were triggered by her marital difficulties. At a young age, she, too, had been deeply wounded by her father, this time due to neglect. To compensate, she set about trying to please him, so that he might notice her efforts and pay more attention to her. Later in life, this behavior turned into looking for a man who would play the role of the attentive father she longed for. Moving from one relationship to another, she saw all men as people she needed to please and take care of, never thinking of herself, hoping unconsciously to get her "father's" approval.

Upon meeting her husband, she found someone who promised to play the part perfectly. He had the right combination of fatherliness, someone with power whose approval would mean something to her, while at the same time demonstrating a great need for her help—he had a severe addiction to marijuana and alcohol. She was fully seduced by his initial display of attention for her, though with his addictions, he was not truly able to consider her needs beyond his own. This would keep her in the game of trying to get his love, a personality style which had become her strategy for living. Without it, she said, "I wouldn't know who I was." This provided the theatrical stage for both of them to play out their scripts for many years.

As I made this interpretation to her, she realized that she had unwittingly been relating to her husband as though he were her father. Her unconscious began to open. A dream during this time in her therapy revealed her progress: A huge insect [in the dream it was called a "Staghorn"—clearly a male symbol] was on her back with "claws" dug deeply into her. She had to bear its weight on her shoulders. The symbolism was obvious. Then, another insect appeared, equally large, but this time a beautiful moth, walking on its own in front of her. This was the portent of a new vision of men for her, and a new way for her to relate to them. The moth also symbolized her own transformation, from undeveloped larva to something beautiful which could fly.

At the peak of her process, she projected her feelings about men upon me as well. It had always been difficult for her to show her need for my approval, just as she felt compelled to put on a pleasing front for her father. One day in a session, she literally started seeing her father's face superimposed upon mine, as her self-perception became that of a very small child. My voice grew farther and farther away to her as she relived the distancing of her father. She began to see herself getting smaller and smaller and becoming progressively more afraid of me. I encouraged her to express herself, and the tears came bursting forth with "Daddy, Daddy, I need you." Then huge anger, a lifetime of anger, at his not having been there for her. And finally, peace, surrender, quiet.

She had found and faced her core fear of never getting her father's approval. As she did so, her perception shifted accordingly, and she saw him for who he was. More importantly, she could see herself for who she was, no longer a needy and fearful "daughter," but a powerful, regal woman. Looking in the mirror, she saw her beauty and her love, free from the need to please others in order to win their love in return, and free to express her love in ways and with people where it could be truly given and received. Today, she is no longer doubting herself but has learned to call her husband on his manipulations. He has entered AA as a result, and their communication has taken on new levels of truth and mutual discovery. She is preparing now to find her life's work, her "soul work," in the healing arts, expressing the power she has found within.

## Tom and Barbara

The core fear and chief defense dictate our general response to life as well as the very specific decisions we make, usually in unconsciousness. Here is a story of a man who had no idea that the job he chose was completely determined by his core fear and chief defense.

Tom, an employee at a major airline, remembered a time in childhood when his babysitter took him to church. They arrived late and were forced to go to the front pew, where the only two open seats were available. The babysitter was grossly overweight so that Tom felt terribly embarrassed at having to walk to the front for all to see. To make matters worse, the babysitter was so large that she required both seats and Tom was forced to sit on the floor, again, for all to see. These many years later he realized why he took the job he had: He was responsible for making sure every passenger who booked a flight with the airline got the seat they needed!

The core fear-chief defense dynamic also has us endlessly recreating the same scenario that gave rise to them in the first place. Here is the story of Barbara, age 65, who uncovered the experience that led to a lifetime of "taking care of things."

When Barbara was very young, her mother felt it was too much responsibility to take care of her, and left her with a great-aunt. Barbara was terrified of this woman, and at only six years of age, she ran away from her in the middle of winter. Having been shown the way from her mother's house to her great-aunt's house only once before, she nevertheless walked the three miles with her dog to find her mother. When she got there, scared and cold, she found her great-aunt there as well, ready to take her back. Running to her mother and clinging to her skirt, Barbara begged her to let her stay. When finally her mother relented, Barbara discovered her ability, if she took care of things, to make herself safe.

She married at age 15, finding a husband who needed her to take care of him, adding to her sense of being able to ensure her safety by "taking care of things." She had five children to take care of by the age of 25. An incredibly hard worker, she began her own business breeding and selling exotic reptiles. Now she had hundreds of animals that needed her to take care of them twenty-four hours a day, seven days a week.

When she came to my office, she was burned out from a lifetime of responsibility. But despite repeated attempts to help her face her fear, letting go of control and asking others to pick up the slack, she would continue in her role as caretaker.

Shortly thereafter, she learned that she had contracted a rare disease from working with the reptiles. If she did not give up the business, she would die. If nothing else, I thought, this would be the catalyst for her letting go of her chief defense. Instead, she acted as if saving the business was more important than her health. It was, she said, her only way of providing for her family and taking care of things. When I pointed out that if she were to die, she wouldn't be around to take care of anything, she said with resignation, "Maybe it isn't worth living, then."

Realizing the thickness of her defense, I was forced to go back to the origin of her core fear. She had become inured to her fears with a defense of strength that had turned into callousness about her life; this strength was built on a weakness, a fear, that could not face reality. If she were to be helped, we could only go back to the original fear, causing an eruption from her depths that could break through the crust she had sealed herself shut with.

Reliving the feelings of the original scene at six years old, she shed her first tear since that time. Softening the hard edges of her personality, she is slowly learning to feel her vulnerability. I have been working with her husband as well, helping him to assume his responsibility for nurturing and taking care of his wife, allowing her to feel her femininity for the first time and rely on his strength to take care of things as appropriate. Together, they are revamping their business, taking her out of danger and finding new ways to provide for their financial and emotional needs.

## The Problem of Defensiveness

The strategy of the core fear and chief defense, as a way to make life work, always backfires. While promising to keep us safe, it actually makes true Joy impossible. With our core fear as a warning system, we believe our chief defense will protect our Joy. The problem is, while preoccupied with fear, we cannot relax to enjoy the protection it is supposed to bring.

A prison guard is as much a prisoner as is his charge while he has to keep watch over him. We cannot truly be free while having to protect ourselves against that which can take away our freedom. The moment we relax, the threat looms again, like a Sword of Damocles always ready to drop.

In this way, we lose sight of the real meaning of Joy, mistaking the means for the end. Our defense was meant to be a tool for recapturing Joy. Instead, we have become devoted to the defense; we worship it and make sacrifice to it. We are compelled by the core fear to exercise our defense over and over again. No matter how many times it has not brought us Joy, we are convinced that just one more try will do the trick. Insanity, as the popular definition goes, is repeating the same thing over and over again, each time expecting different results. This is the constant dirge we sing; just one more attempt to make illusions real and somehow we will succeed. Instead, we suffer each time the strategy fails, and we are bitterly disappointed. Like rearranging the deck chairs on the *Titanic*, we occupy ourselves with an illusion of productivity while our ship is sinking.

The moment we decide that fear is something real needing our defense, we begin living in a fearful world. Even though our defense may seem to be successful, it requires that our attention be on fear so we may defend against it. This locks us into a mind-set of fear and we are lost to Joy. We have long ago become stuck in this pattern and, too afraid to give up the defense, simply go on automatic pilot. One patient, upon seeing the futility of defensiveness, described it as "a loyal dog lying down beside its dead master."

A Chinese proverb states, "We are always waiting to live." And we wait for the rest of our lives. We know that our defense can never bring real Joy. But still we wait, hoping for a new solution, one where we can have the Joy we've been seeking without having to give up our defense or face the fear it was hiding. This is the source of suffering; this is how we create our own hell.

## Bypassing the Chief Defense

We may now understand the principle of finding and facing fear at its deeper level: The solution to our problems lies in finding and facing the core fear *through bypassing the chief defense.* This means either doing nothing to attempt to protect ourselves from fear or actively doing the opposite of what the defense says to do. And as we have seen, doing this has us realize the great truth that leads inevitably to Joy—that which has been chasing us all our lives is not real as we had imagined it to be. The choices we made and the circumstances in which we made them have little or no bearing on who we are today. While the chief defense kept us from even looking at other choices, we have lived as if the circumstances in which we made them were still going on. Our personality was frozen at the moment we first defended ourselves, and we have been imagining the same threat is still looming above us, ready to pounce. Until we bypass the chief defense, we replay these circumstances over and over, dancing the dance of fear. Caught on this treadmill, we are convinced that something terrible will happen if we stop.

As with Medusa, who must be seen only in the shield's reflection, we are certain we will be turned to stone if we look fear straight in the eye. When we summon the courage to face our demons, we find instead they hold a gift for us, and the gift is the discovery that when we face them, they dissolve into nothingness. With this, we learn of our true stature, our spiritual power, and our freedom from all fear that would bind us.

But to discover this, we must be willing to short-circuit the defense that keeps us from our fear. As long as we exercise our defense, we cannot get close enough to the fear to see if it is real or not. That we are so insistent it is real when we have not examined it for ourselves makes no sense. And why would we fight this when it is the key to release from our unhappiness? Let us instead hope that it is true, "hope we have been wrong," to find the willingness to face the fear and discover for ourselves that it has no bite.

When the pain is great enough, we will risk facing our fear. But we may spare ourselves this pain, speeding up the time of Joy, by realizing that our strategy of protection, our unwillingness to face fear, is the very cause of our pain. Our only need, then, is courage and a passionate desire for Joy. We must dare not to respond to fear with defense. We must dare not to repeat this endless loop, declaring instead that we no longer believe in fear's power over us. When we find out that indeed no harm comes, our conviction is fortified and we discover our release. In this way we may recreate ourselves, redesign our lives, and freely *choose* our way of being in the world. Herein lies the secret to radical Joy!

## EXERCISES

### Exercise 1: Discovering Your Core Fear

This is the centerpiece of the path to Joy, the basic foundation of our program. The enormous power that comes through knowing your core fear is not to be underestimated. It literally holds the promise of changing your life. *Please* work this process over and over until you are sure you have found your core fear, and then work it some more! It will become the primary tool in your dealing effectively with life on an ongoing basis.

The process in which we are about to engage will expose the fundamental workings of your unconscious. Beginning with a problem, the successive layers of fear will be revealed, until the core is reached. At bottom, we are all afraid of losing our "individuality," our separateness, and the chance to make reality what we wish.

To begin, pick some problem in your life, some fear creating troubling circumstances. It does not matter which problem you pick; all problems lead to the core fear—they are but the core fear in one of its many disguises. The core fear is always some universal theme of loss:—abandonment, pain (really, the fear of what the pain will lead to), death, loss of identity (the need for full self-expression), loss of freedom, loss of meaning, etc. Each of these, in truth, is but a disguise for the one basic fear, the granddaddy of them all, the fear of returning to Oneness.

Write out your problem in a short sentence on the left side of the first line on your paper. On the right side, write down a specific question to help you find the fear *underneath* the problem you've just described. There are three forms of this question—choose whichever one is most helpful to you for finding the answer. The three questions to ask in response to the problem you've written down are:

1. "Why is this upsetting to me?"
2. "What am I afraid will happen next?"
3. "What am I afraid I will miss or lose?"

Write one of these questions on the right side of the paper then record your answer to this question on the left side, underneath the first line. This answer will describe a new problem, a new fear. Make sure you write it in a short, concise sentence. Again, choose one of the three questions to ask of this new problem and write it on the right side of of your paper. Continue this process until you reach the core fear.

You will know when you have reached the core when you have a sense of deep recognition, an "aha!", and often, an emotional release. Review the list of core fears above to understand the universal quality of the core fear; in later exercises you will see how it applies to every aspect of your life. Look for a feeling of "Yes, this is what's been going on underneath it all, my entire life." Also, look for spontaneous memories of some of the situations which involved your core fear.

Here is an example of an actual session of finding the core fear. The subject—we'll call him John—started out thinking he had no fears. However, one of John's fears was of *admitting* to himself that he had them.

| Fear | Question |
|---|---|
| 1. I'm afraid to commit to my girlfriend and marry her. | Why is this upsetting to me? |
| 2. If I marry her, I'll feel trapped. | What am I afraid will happen next? |
| 3. I won't get a chance to do what I want in life. | What am I afraid I will miss or lose? |
| 4. I'd lose the chance to find true meaning. | Why is that upsetting to me? |
| 5. I'll never be completely fulfilled. | What am I afraid will happen next? |
| 6. My life would be empty. | Why is that upsetting to me? |
| 7. It feels like I wouldn't count. | What am I afraid I will miss or lose? |
| 8. I feel this incredible passion, this love for life, and I want to share that and make a difference. I'd never get to do that. | |

At this point, John's eyes began to fill up and he later reported thinking of his childhood, where he felt very loved and very happy. He spontaneously realized that he had been wanting to recapture this feeling and share it with the world, and that this had driven his major decisions, in his career (he was a social worker), his spirituality, and now his potential marriage.

John's core fear was of losing his identity, of not expressing himself fully in life, and he now could see it operating the machinery of his decision making throughout his life.

Sally, a woman who was driven by the need to please people, went through the process this way:

| Fear | Question |
|------|----------|
| 1. I feel guilty about having told my friend I can't go out with her tonight. | Why is this upsetting to me? |
| 2. I'm afraid she might be mad at me. | Why is that upsetting to me? |
| 3. She might bad-mouth me to other people. | What am I afraid will happen next? |
| 4. People would start talking about me. | What am I afraid I will miss or lose? |
| 5. I'd lose my friends. | What am I afraid will happen next? |
| 6. I'd be lonely. | Why is this upsetting to me? |
| 7. I'd never have the chance to share my love; life would be empty and gray, no more fun, no more joy. Just empty. | |

This is the core fear of abandonment. All core fears interrelate; Sally is also afraid that she will lose her identity if she cannot share her love. This can even be said to be the fear of death, the final abandonment, for fear says that, with death, we will never again have the chance to express ourselves.

As you perform the core fear exercise, keep in mind these important tips:

- Use a pencil with a big eraser! You'll want to refine your answers over and over until you are crystal clear on the core fear.
- Keep your answers short and very specific. Our fear loves abstraction. It doesn't want us to face it and can therefore make us masterfully vague!
- State your fear in a way that you can ask one of the three questions. For example, if you answer the question "Why is fighting with my spouse upsetting to me?" by re-

sponding "Because I like peace," you cannot then ask, "Why is peace upsetting to me?" Rather, you want to state the answer in the form of a fear, such as "Because I will lose peace." It might be helpful to state the fear in the form of "If [your fear from the previous line], then [your new fear]." For example, if the question is "Why is fighting with my spouse upsetting to me?," you might state the answer as "If I fight with my spouse, then I will lose peace."

- Don't worry if an answer to one of the questions seems ridiculous or obvious. You may say to yourself, "Why is the fear of losing my job upsetting to me? Who wouldn't be upset by that?" Stick with the process and answer it as clearly as you possibly can. The answer tells something very specific about *you;* even if everyone might have the same answer, the memories it triggers in you tell how you learned to be afraid of it.

- Be on the lookout for the "repetitive loop," where the answer you give to one of the three questions is actually a restatement of the previous answer, worded differently. For example: "Why is fighting with my spouse upsetting to me? Because I don't like fighting" actually restates the same problem and doesn't go to the next step. You need to get underneath this layer of the fear, getting closer to the core by really seeing why the one answer is upsetting to you, or what you are afraid will happen *next,* or what you are afraid you will miss or lose if the first answer occurred. "Fighting with my spouse is upsetting to me because I'm afraid he or she will leave me" is taking the process to the next level.

- The whole problem with fear is that we don't want to look at it. Above all else, if you want to find your Joy, be willing to look at your fear! It is perfectly safe; you will not make it come true by looking at it. In fact, you will see it for the illusion it is. It is impossible to overstress the importance of staying with this exercise until you reach the core. Keep looking for why it is upsetting to you, play out the scenario in your mind, and see what you imagine will happen next or what you will miss or lose. Keep digging until you hit gold!

## Exercise 2: Revealing Your Chief Defense

Each of us devises a specific way of dealing with fear. This was established when we first encountered our core fear and found a way to make ourselves safe from it. This defense style becomes our strategy for living, a guiding plan that we have been using to succeed in life ever since. It is our way of avoiding capture by the core fear. We can have no real success in finding Joy while our chief defense rests in obscurity, dictating our path and keeping us enslaved to it. To face our fear is the key to Freedom. Therefore, we must find the chief defense which keeps us from facing our fear, so that we may bypass it and move through the fear to the other side.

To find our chief defense, we may either look at how we respond to fear in the present or go back to the origin of our core fear and see how we responded then. In fact, each response to fear in the present is a recapitulation of what happened at the beginning.

In this exercise, we will go back to the past and see how it is being reenacted in the present every time we are faced with fear and have a decision to make.

### First Memory of the Core Fear

Start a new page in your Workbook titled "First Memory of the Core Fear," and write down the earliest memory you can recall where you experienced your core fear. Searching your memory, opening up your unconscious, creates a hypnotic state which is much more powerful if written down or talked out than if simply performed in your head alone. Write down, in as much detail as possible, the events surrounding your earliest memory of the core fear. You may recall the origin of it. If not, that's fine. Just go back as far as you are able, even if it's only yesterday. The farther back you can go, the better, simply because you were less defended earlier on; defenses grow stronger over time until life experience or conscious effort begins to crack their shell.

Remember this early incident in as much detail as possible. Really take yourself back there. Remember the sights, sounds, smells, tastes, and touches that were present at that time; remember the feelings you had, the physical sensation of those feelings. Remember the things that were said, and the things that were done. How did you feel each step of the way? Out of control? Lost? Angry? Helpless? Scared? Confused? As you remember all this, think in the language you would have thought at that time. Perhaps it is so long ago that you did not have verbal language and your memory is based purely on sensory knowing. Whatever your situation, play out the scene *as if you were there now* and bring it back to life.

### Response to the Core Fear

Next, staying in the hypnotic state as you continue to remember, write down the answers to the following questions under the heading "Response to the Core Fear."

What response did you come up with to make yourself safe from the fear? Look for the promise you made, something you committed to doing, so that you would never have to face those feelings again. How did you handle this situation? What did you do in the midst of your fear to take care of it? Notice how you reacted, what thoughts you had, what you said and did, how you felt when you did these things. What did you do to make this intolerable situation tolerable? What brought relief? Safety? Control? Look very carefully for all the subtleties of what you found that took care of your fear and set you on a road of feeling safe and whole again.

## Response to Fears Today

Next, think about how you now deal with problems, crises, danger, the possibility of threat. Find the basic way you respond to fear in the present. Consider what you typically do to try to handle a variety of situations and then look for the strategy underlying them all. Do you give up, get angry, ask for help, do it yourself? Are you a perfectionist, avoiding potential problems by making certain everything is done exactly right? What do you do when someone gets angry at you? Do you people-please, get angry back, try to overpower them? Do you caretake, become selfish or self-interested, say "nothing bothers me," become hypervigilant for threat, become helpless (waiting for or demanding that someone take care of you), become depressed, or exercise a "spiritual bypass"? What do you do when obstacles arise? Do you try to rescue people in trouble? Do you take on the role of provider? Look also at the problems you currently have and see how you are in some way trying to engineer a particular outcome, using your best ideas for how to succeed. All of these are spin-offs of your chief defense, how you dealt with your core fear the first time it erupted. Write the answers to these questions under the heading "Response to fears today."

## Coming Up with the Chief Defense

Finally, look for the connection between your responses to the core fear and your response to fears today. Can you see the way today's responses are derivative of the response of long ago? Keep looking for the connection (you may want to try different wordings of the response to your core fear) and come up with a one-line description of your overall response. This is your chief defense. Write it under the heading "Chief defense."

## Sample

John, in the "core fear" example above, filled out the chart in the following way. Notice how these fears and defenses led to his present concern about whether to marry his girlfriend.

### First Memory of the Core Fear

When I was fourteen, I remember going to my parents for help with sorting out some powerful feelings I was having, with questions about "Who am I?" and "How can I find real meaning?" They had always been able to answer and take care of everything, so when they simply smiled with love but didn't really understand my problem, I was extremely upset. They couldn't help me for the first time and I was alone; I no longer had my secure world. I felt like I was staring into a void of nothingness, with nothing to hold on to for a sense of who I was.

### Response to the Core Fear

I went back to my room and began writing notes about my feelings. The relief that this brought, as I was able to put down on paper what I couldn't communicate to my parents, was incredible! I became bent on finding the answers to my pain in this way, thinking almost obsessively and writing notes. I wouldn't let a single thought go by that held some important insight without writing it down. Each thought held a piece of the answer to life's problems. I was going to coordinate these notes in a single "magnum opus" and give it to the world. This would help everyone, I believed, and they would love me for it. This is how I hoped to get my world back, the world I knew before the fear began.

*Response to Fears Today*

I become preoccupied with finding ways to control the thing I'm afraid of, especially with how to get other people's love and approval. I obsess a bit about that. I'm also, still, very philosophical, trying to figure things out to comfort myself when I'm afraid. The thinking goes that if I can figure things out well enough, if I get very analytical, I can understand any problem and gain control over it. Control is a big thing for me. I'm fastidious about keeping things organized, to prevent problems from happening in the first place. I worry a lot about things that might get out of my control, like health problems, money problems and the like.

*Chief Defense*

Control or perfectionism, either way of describing it. I see now that I've been trying to get back the secure, "perfect" world of my childhood.

## Exercise 3: Creating Your Life Journey

Now that you have found your core fear and chief defense, let us see how they have built your personality, setting the twists and turns of your life and driving all of your actions and goals.

### Time Line of Life Events

On a fresh sheet (or sheets) in your Workbook, make a series of rows representing the years of your life, and number them from "0" to your present age. In the space next to each appropriate age, write a short phrase that characterizes the significant happenings of that year, chronicling the events that shaped your life's direction. Go through each year of your life and see what decisions you had to make, what influences took place, what events or crises occurred, big or small. If you feel they had an impact on the course of your life, write them down.

Be as thorough as you can, really reviewing each year for any important occurrences, decisions, life changes. Ask for help with the early years from those who knew you. You are doing a life review and you want to enter into the hypnotic memory, reliving these events as if they were happening to you now, as completely as possible.

Notice how each event contained some fear: If there was a decision to be made, perhaps you feared the consequences of making a wrong choice. If there were subtle but important influences, perhaps you feared the change in your identity, not knowing who you would be. Perhaps it was simply the next phase of life which contained a fear of the unknown. Even positive events, such as marriage or going to college, can cause fear of the unknown, and we may respond, however wisely, from our chief defense.

## Flowchart for Your Life Journey

Next we will create the "Flowchart for Your Life Journey." At the top and center of a new page in your notebook, write down the earliest event on your time line that describes the first confrontation with your core fear. Draw a box around it. Now draw a line coming out from the bottom of this box, and alongside the line write down the way you responded to the event. This response was your chief defense, the first time you discovered and used it. At the end of this line, draw another box and write inside the next event on your time line which resulted from this response. You have now created a connection between your core fear, the chief defense which arose from it, and the life situation which resulted.

Let's look at an example. Jessica, a 63-year-old client, remembered the events which first gave rise to her core fear. When she was seven years old, her father lost his job and the family had to move to a new neighborhood. At a particularly vulnerable time in her development, she was uprooted from everything familiar—her friends, her house, the life she had known and loved. When her mother fell into depression, withdrawing from the family, Jessica's loss became too much for her to bear.

Her chief defense arose in that moment: If her mother could withdraw from her, she would withdraw from her mother, and from everyone, to protect herself from the pain of this loss. If she didn't involve herself with people, she reasoned, she wouldn't be vulnerable to such pain again.

In creating her flowchart, Jessica wrote in the first box: "We moved; my mother withdrew from us" (see diagram below). On the line coming out from this box, she wrote down her chief defense: "I withdrew from people." Out of this line came the box which described the next event on her time line: "I began to fail in school." She understood that the failing in school was a direct result of her withdrawal from people, as she said to herself, "I don't need anybody, including my teachers and classmates."

After completing the first connection on your flowchart, repeat the process, drawing a line out from the box you have just filled in and writing your response alongside it. This represents your "second-generation" defense, the chief defense tailored to the new circumstances. Connect this with the next event on your time line. Again, identify the cause-effect relationship between your defense and the resulting event.

Of course, there may be more than one event which followed from your defensive response. If this is the case, create a branching line out from the first box (see diagram below) and connect it to all the boxes which contain the resulting events. For Jessica, the line stating "I withdrew from people" branched out to two boxes: "I began to fail in school" and "I stopped playing with friends."

Out from each of these boxes, draw lines to connect with the next set of boxes, creating new branches as necessary. Alongside these lines, write down your defensive responses as well. For example, out of the box that said, "I began to fail in school," came a line on which Jessica wrote, "I told myself school didn't matter" (a second-generation defense built on "I don't need anyone"). This line led to a box that said, "The guidance counselor at school took me under her wing." Out of the box which said, "I stopped playing with friends," came a line that said, "I found solace with animals," leading to the box: "My father got me a dog." These separate branches eventually led to her interest in animal rights (coming from her defense of taking comfort from and feeling needed by animals instead of people) and to her profession as a veterinarian.

Continue the lines and boxes as long as necessary to come to the present day, tracing the fear and defense patterns that elaborate who you are now and how you got here.

This flowchart is a picture of your life, the events and decisions which built your personality and helped you become who you are today. How much does your life seem to have been run for you, choices made unconsciously by the core fear and chief defense? How much would you like to choose your course consciously, steering clear of old patterns and disappointing results, actively creating your Joy?

For a real eye-opener, start out with the same flowchart, but at a certain row, choose another response you could have made to the situation, something other than that which your defense required. Imagine what consequences might have resulted from this change and write them in the boxes beneath this line. There are always an infinite number of ways to respond to any situation. Part of the miracle of facing your core fear without responding to it from the chief defense is that you suddenly see these many options. Fill in the subsequent lines and boxes to see who you might have been had you taken this course. It is these responses that determine the structure of our lives, not the circumstances we find ourselves in. Any new moment gives us the chance to "choose once again" and create a new life, a new personality, and a new world around us.

## Sample Flowchart for Jessica

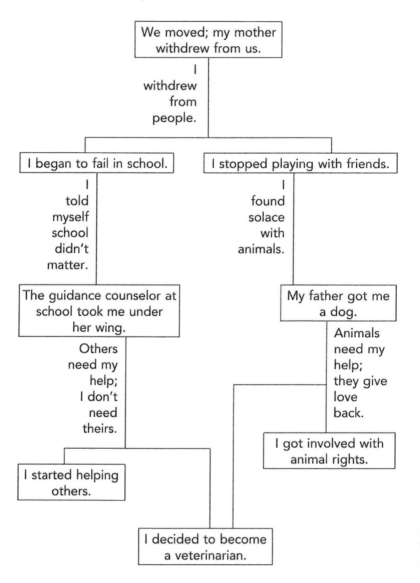

# PART II

# THREE DOORWAYS TO JOY: MIND, BODY, AND SPIRIT

# INTRODUCTION

# THE STRATEGIC APPROACH TO JOY

In the search for fulfillment, our task is to shift our focus from fear to Joy, choosing where we place our attention. As we shine the spotlight on our chosen view, we bring that reality into existence—that becomes the world we see. This moment of choice offers a "crack between the worlds," an opening through which we may enter and assume our rightful place as the creators of our experience.

There are three approaches to this opening, three "doorways to Joy": the doorways of the mind, body, and spirit. We will now explore each of these in depth, fashioning our world along the principles of choice, discovering our Joy as we do so.

The most direct route to Joy is through the doorway of the spirit, where we become so invigorated by a joyful and high Purpose that the attraction of fear pales by comparison.

When the glitter of fear continues to sparkle more brilliantly for us, drawing our attention away from Joy, we must sort out the thoughts fueling the fear and discover them to be illusory. This is the doorway of the mind.

When even this effort is overwhelmed by our feeling of threat, we must work out the fear in its physical form through the doorway of the body. Here we discharge the muscular tension built from stored fear, energized by our thoughts and projected onto the body.

In truth, all three are but variations on the same theme: finding and facing our fear to watch it dissolve into illusion. For in the end, all three must work together, regardless of which doorway was opened first, for a complete transformation. Discharging the physical energy of fear brings a deep relaxation and peace which organizes our thoughts and opens the spirit. Working through the thoughts of fear effects this same physical relaxation while removing that which obstructs awareness of the spirit. And finding a transcendent spiritual perspective automatically creates order in the mind and healing of the body, as they are no longer used to serve fear's agenda but reflect the Joy now recognized on all levels.

While all three approaches are ultimately the same, still we must be strategic about which we choose, and when. The path can be fraught with pitfalls. Fear comes in many subtle forms and can distort our perception of a true path. We can even be motivated by a hidden fear in choosing which doorway to enter. It is important, then, to be aware of the many false strategies—manifestations of fear in disguise—which can lead us astray or cause us to sink into quicksand, as we open up these doorways.

The first of the false strategies for Joy is the "ostrich approach," or burying one's head in the sand. In this strategy, we are unwilling even to look at fear in order to transform it. We refuse to open any of the doors. Not only does this make transformation impossible, but it runs the risk of repression as we actively bury the fear where it continues its work underground. This is a false approach to the doorway of the mind which proposes that we choose not to think the thoughts of fear, pretending they are not there, as a solution to our problems. Of course, with our head in the sand, the problem comes up to hit us on the backside.

In a similar way, there are those who demonstrate a "spiritual ungroundedness," where in their zeal for Enlightenment and Joy, they look only at the lofty and the beautiful. The tragic mistake in this is the refusal to look at the so-called "base" and "unbeautiful," so that it, too, may be recognized for the Joy it hides.

A close cousin to this trap is the "denial of the body" (and the world). Here, we believe that if we can get past the body's pulls and urges, if we can steel ourselves against them, we can be free from their demands and pursue the Joy we want instead. As the Buddha discovered in his philosophy of "the middle way," this perpetuates and magnifies the fear of the body's impulses, not truly transforming them. And as Kahlil Gibran says in *The Prophet*, "You can muffle the drum, and you can loosen the strings of the lyre, but who shall command the skylark not to sing?" Our journey to Joy is not about denying anything, but rather finding the music within it all; it is about revealing rather than concealing, including rather than censoring.

"Intellectualism," a thin disguise for fear, wears the cover of "mind as the only doorway," and clearly hides the fear of contact with the body and the spirit.

If our path to Joy becomes too struggle-filled, if we are working too hard without enough reward, then we can stumble into the next pitfall called "losing heart." This pitfall is often compensated for with a strategy of "Be content with less." For this, two things are necessary: To seek and find some spiritual fulfillment in a form which energizes and reinvigorates the soul (especially drawing on the support of others, a spiritual community), and to recognize (with the doorway of the mind) that the thought "the path is difficult" is but a product of the core fear.

Next is "the paralysis of indecision." This pitfall comes from a strategy that advises "If you don't make any decision, you avoid making a wrong decision." It is another distortion of the doorway of the mind. The problem is overcome when we discover that even an imperfect choice is better than no choice. For this, we must find the core fear at work. We may then release it with the understanding that it is not really a question of which choice to make, but a fear of the responsibility that comes with making any choice.

Then there is the problem of "impatience." The fear that says "I must have it now" becomes the very thing which interferes with our success. Our solution lies in the infinite expansiveness of the spirit which can hold such impatience in its larger context.

Finally, there is the pitfall of "insisting on being right instead of happy." This, as we have seen, results when "saving face" becomes more important than Joy. We hold fast to the mind's idea of how to stay safe from fear by building ourself up in the eyes of others.

In summary, we must be strategic in our approach to Joy, using whichever combination of the three doorways is most appropriate and effective. Generally, we want to remember that the doorway of the spirit is the fastest and most direct route to Joy, the doorway of the mind is next, and the doorway of the body is third.

Do not, however, let this order become a roadblock itself, convincing you that you must only travel through the doorway of the spirit because it is more "pure" or because it is the fastest. What is fastest and "best" is what works most effectively! Again, if your fear has you too much in its grip, preventing you from rising above it into a spiritual perspective, then you want to work out the fear-thoughts first. With this, your ascension will be natural and full of grace. If your thoughts are too scrambled and you are buzzing with fear, then discharge the energy of it from your body. The relaxation and detachment this brings is a most beautiful way to take back command of your thoughts and expand into the spirit. Because all three doorways are so intimately connected—the spirit energizing the thoughts which then project onto the body— all three become one in their resolution of fear and the return of Joy.

# CHAPTER 4

# THE DOORWAY OF THE MIND

One day long ago, in ancient Japan, a fiercesome samurai approached a peaceful monk in his monastery. He ordered the monk in a booming voice, "Monk, teach me about heaven and hell." The monk sized him up and looked him over and finally said, "Teach *you* about heaven and hell? I couldn't teach you anything! You're filthy, you smell, your sword is rusty ... you are a disgrace to the samurai!" Filled with rage, the warrior drew his sword and was readying to strike the monk down dead. Quietly, the monk said, "That's hell." The samurai was taken aback, stopping in his tracks. Realizing that this little monk was willing even to sacrifice his life to teach him the meaning of hell, he slowly began lowering his sword and was filled with a strange and overwhelming peace. Whereupon the monk said softly, "That's heaven."

—Source unknown

Betty, a 49-year-old housewife, was unhappy in her marriage. She came to my office complaining that her husband did not honor or respect her. Her feelings, she said, were not being considered, her needs not being met.

Although the presentation of her problem seemed sincere, something struck me as "not quite right" about it. I didn't doubt that she believed wholeheartedly what she was saying, but it seemed to me that her husband's behavior did not warrant the type of response she was having. I sniffed a core fear at work.

Searching for this core fear, I asked Betty why her husband's lack of respect bothered her. She answered, "Because I feel like I won't be heard." I then asked her why not being heard was upsetting to her. "Because I feel powerless to get my needs met," she replied. And what was she afraid would happen if she didn't get her needs met? "I feel like I'll die." At this point, she took on the demeanor of a very young girl, with tears in her eyes and a look of great insecurity. I asked her what she was experiencing. It was then that the memory of her mother's "death act" resurfaced.

Betty was 4 years old the first time she remembers her mother playing dead on the floor. This was a tactic her mother would use to get the children to cooperate and "be good." At such a young age, Betty was terrified of her power to make her mother live or die.

She learned to be careful and dutiful. Whatever her mother asked, she would do. Still, there were times when her mother would drop to the floor, her children in tears around her, not knowing what they had done. Betty's response was to plead with and beg her mother to come back to life, with promises that she would be good. This worked; if Betty importuned with enough force, her mother would indeed come back to life.

These were the first moments of her core fear and chief defense, the ingredients of a strategy for living that would become her personality. She would learn to wear an attitude of dutiful compliance that would keep her mother alive and well.

As she grew older, she generalized her strategy to include anyone she needed or depended upon. If, however, she met someone who responded differently, she would become intensely angry and demanding, not understanding why her strategy had failed her. Such was the case with her husband. It was at these times that she came in contact with the feelings she would like to have expressed to her mother, but did not dare for fear of her demise. Her anger served as both a "second line of defense" to control her "mother's" behavior, as well as the release of stored feelings for never having had her needs met.

We explored, in her "Life Journey," how this dynamic had been playing out through the years. Growing up, she became a "caretaker," especially with her mother and others who would play the helpless role. She married her first husband at age 17, attempting to relieve herself of this burden. Terribly disappointed by her father's unwillingness to rescue her from her mother, Betty sought out and found a man who would.

For a while, she was happy. But soon her husband began to abuse her, leaving home for days at a time to have affairs with other women. He would beat her upon his return, angry at her for making him feel guilty because of her goodness and compliance.

Finally, having had enough, she stopped being so dutiful and began doing more for herself. When another man showed interest in her, she became embroiled, through no fault of her own, in a love triangle. Angry and self-destructive, her husband began a fight with this man, which ended up in her husband's death. Betty's core fear was reignited: If only she had remained dutiful, she thought, this would not have happened, her husband would not have been killed. This recapitulated the circumstances which gave birth to Betty's core fear—that she had the power to make people live or die. She felt her husband's death was her fault.

At the appropriate time in our work together, I took Betty through a session of Transpersonal Breathwork, a powerful tool that gives access to the unconscious and transpersonal domains. In her experience, she went back to this episode of her life. She envisioned herself trying to crawl into the coffin with her husband by way of doing penance to him for her terrible deed. At a later workshop, a psychodramatic scene was set up to allow her to see, in physical form, how her mother and husband had been living in her mind throughout her life. But this time she would rewrite the script, creating a new ending. With strong support from the group, and a commitment to living her own life, she literally turned her back on the people playing the roles of her mother and husband, releasing herself from their influence.

The difficulty she had in facing her fear and letting go was evidence of the depth to which the fear had her in its clutches. Finally, it came down to either their life or hers. With a tremendous emotional release and huge expression of her power, she had turned her back and allowed them to die (in her mind). Now free from her core fear, she was able to see how it had her endlessly repeating the thought at its source—that it was her responsibility to make people live or die, to make them happy or unhappy, and so on. She could see how her pattern of compliance alternating with anger arose from these imprints and how it had dictated her important life decisions. This insight gave her the courage to change those aspects of her life which were not serving her, and create a new way of relating to others.

Today, she is discovering a fulfillment and an ease in her relationship with her new husband, the one with whom she had been so demanding and by whom she had felt so unheard. Their relationship reflects the Joy of two people coming together in their wholeness. She has sought out and found employment for the first time in her life, wanting to make her own way, free from childhood dependencies. Finally, she exudes the inner peace and quiet confidence of a woman who knows herself and has no fear of being disrespected.

## Constructing the Human Experience

All of our human experience begins with thought. We know the world only through the thoughts we choose to have about it. The many aspects of human-being-ness are, at their root, spin-offs of the choice to think with the mind of either fear or Joy.

These thoughts then project outwardly as perception, the

great architect of reality. Perception literally constructs our sensory experience according to the blueprints of our chosen thoughts. And until our perception is fully joyful, it is the core fear and chief defense which provide the foundation of all our thinking. In adopting our core fear and chief defense early in life, we learn to perceive everything through their filters. What we perceive reflects back to us what we have chosen to think about it.

Having projected our thoughts as perception, we then assign meaning to the world. The circumstances of our lives are given the meaning they have according to whether they promote or protect against our core fear. That is, we assign their meaning according to whether they will keep us safe and promote our Joy or threaten it in some way.

Upon giving meaning to the circumstances of our world, we give meaning to ourselves. We develop our sense of identity, our personality, along the lines of what these phenomena mean to us. All of our behavior—physical, mental, and emotional—is informed by such meanings. We *become* the kind of person who will respond to these meanings in the way our defenses dictate. We become the kind of person who will see ourselves as threatened or protected by the situation in our unique way. Everything we encounter from that moment forward is understood as either preserving and promoting our sense of self or attacking it in some way.

This is the variety of human experience—the arrogance of war, the despair of loneliness, the pain of a broken heart, and the fear of illness and death are given sweeping and profound understanding in this context—they are the cause and effect, the woof and warp of our strategy to stay safe from threat and to secure our Good.

Betty's story is a powerful demonstration of the link between the choice for fear and the perception that builds the world we see. Betty was living her life based on the thought that she had to ensure that her mother and others would not die. From the earliest moments of its inception, she projected the demands of her core fear—her need for her mother's survival—on to every situation. She literally filtered each experience through this lens, creating the perceptions to which she would then respond and live out her life.

So, too, with the samurai in the opening story of this chapter. Through the monk's teaching, he learned he could choose to see either heaven or hell in the very same circumstances. We will either see through the eyes of Joy or "through a glass darkly." When one is depressed, everything looks empty and devoid of the meaning of Joy. We even say we are "blue." Picasso, when in a period of depression, painted all things he saw under a blue cast. Our perception of the world is literally colored by our ways of thinking.

A patient of mine, after experiencing his first significant release from fear, looked at a painting on the wall in my office, a painting he had seen many times before. Suddenly he exclaimed how vivid the colors were, how beautiful the painting, how he could sink right into and become part of it. He then began looking at me and described the "aura" of light he could see around me. To his surprise, he found he could see the same aura around everything. As he looked at various objects, he described the feeling that the light, the hue, the extra richness of textures and colors which seemed to be emanating from within the "things" of the world outside, were actually reflections of what he was feeling within.

The choice for fear or Joy paints the picture of the world we see. Perception draws its blueprints along the lines of our chosen view, and *everything* takes shape accordingly. When we are not wholly joyous, we may face our fear, challenging the assumptions of the perception we see, and watch as the blueprints are spontaneously erased. The clouds disperse and the light of Joy emerges.

## Imposing Our Wishes upon Reality

In building the perceptual world of separation, we actively, even willfully, push away the experience of Oneness and impose the reality we wish on top of it. This willful activity characterizes the nature of our experience here. In attempting to "real-ize" the separation, we would force all things to comply with our perceptual demands. The world we see, in all of its detail, is but the evidence of the willful denial of Oneness and the imposition of our wishes everywhere we look. We attempt to objectify the separation with a perception that pushes all other experience away.

This, however, creates our problems. Pain is the direct result when reality does not, in fact, comply with our wishes. Indeed it cannot, for the perception of separation makes for an experience where we are cut off from what we really want. But instead of questioning our strategy, we exert our will with renewed intensity, insisting on the reality we would perceive, looking for new ways to reify the separation.

In *Fiddler on the Roof,* Tevye the milkman is invited to the house of Lazar Wolf the butcher. All he is told is that Lazar needs to discuss something "very important" with him. Tevye decides in advance that Lazar wants to buy his milk cow for slaughter. An entire conversation ensues in which Tevye imposes this assumption on top of what Lazar is actually saying. As Lazar talks glowingly about how he has seen "her" many times and how "she has made a big impression" on him, how he'll take care of her and do right by her, finally Tevye realizes he is not talking about the cow at all; he is asking Tevye for his daughter's hand in marriage!

And so it is with perception. Tevye had the fixed idea that Lazar Wolf was up to no good and it colored his perception accordingly. He saw only what he wanted to see and denied the reality before him. How many times have we been angry with someone for a wrong they did not actually commit, or afraid of something that never came to pass?

If we want to end our suffering, we must stop imposing our wishes upon reality. We must withdraw the perceptions we have projected onto reality-as-it-is, and allow ourselves to see things as they truly are. For these perceptions are the messengers of fear, the evidence of separation. It is fear that insists reality comply with our wishes that we may feel safe. To accomplish this, fear projects the perception of what it wants to see and then assigns meaning to the perception. Taking this meaning as "real," we believe we are perceiving "reality." With this, we see ourselves as living in that reality, and our separation from Oneness appears to become actual.

The thought cluster of our fear has us asking in every situation, "Is this going to help or hurt me in protecting against threat and securing my safety?" Tevye saw Lazar through the eyes of his fear, and reacted defensively by deciding he was guilty before giving him a chance. When finally Tevye corrected his perception, he could only laugh at what had previously made him so nervous.

By comparing our situations to the referent of the core fear, we give them a value. We decide how "good" or "bad" something is according to whether it will foster or threaten our wishes. In this way, fear becomes the yardstick by which we measure all things, judge their relative value, and assign their meaning accordingly.

It is in this judging, this assignment of meaning, that we find the moment of choice. Here is the seed thought that blossoms into an entire world of perception. We must now fully explore this moment, so that we may gain mastery over it and develop our skill in transforming it. As you read the next section, even before the exercises which follow, see if you can intuitively feel the fixed grasp of perception loosening, wavering, and ultimately dissolving.

## Something Out of Nothing: The Mechanics of Perception

In our journey out of Oneness, we found projection to be a wonderful instrument. Like a movie projector throwing images on a blank screen, we could impose the reality we wished to see, obscuring reality-as-it-is. The screen is an appropriate metaphor for the undifferentiated Oneness of our original state. Out of this uniform mass, we circumscribe particular shapes, drawing them with our eyes, and declare them to be unique and distinct from the rest. This is the function of perception, to isolate particular forms, like a cookie cutter stamping out shapes on a sheet of dough, from what is otherwise uniform.

In truth, there is no such boundary to identify the form and give it the meaning we perceive. But we deny this fact and see what we will. In this way, we try to "make" reality something we can control in the hope of getting it to conform to our wishes. The world literally takes shape to us as we circumscribe separating lines around "things" to distinguish them from other "things," and then declare them to be real. In so doing, we assign them their value and they take on living meaning to us.

The problem is that we have made up this meaning, and we suffer when the reality we have invented clashes with reality-as-it-is. Again, when we project the reality-we-wish on top of reality-as-it-is, we set up a conflict that must be defended against. In assigning meaning to things, we exercise our power to think independently of reality, to hold our own point of view. And we feel righteously entitled to do so, even when it is in stark contradiction to the way things are. This is how we create our troubles, refusing to accept reality on its own terms, setting ourselves up at war against it.

Our solution lies simply in the realization that we have given arbitrary meaning to all forms. This is the secret of the mystics, for withdrawing such meaning reveals the truth of Oneness behind these forms.

The ability to assign meaning to the many parts of reality gives us a feeling of "authority," as though we were the "authors" of reality. This creates a tremendously addictive thrill, a feeling of power and control after which we lust. It is what hooks us in when we are infants to the worldview of those around us: The looming faces of our parents beseech us to say "Mommy" and "Daddy," and we are well rewarded for our efforts. The lure of buying into the consensual worldview, with its perception of separate identifiers, is strong.

The problem, of course, is that while giving a sense of autonomy and power, it also locks us in to the worldview wherein we are alone; we become one of those separate identifiers! And in this, we become separate from the Oneness, the oceanic bliss we felt before such a division. We are not the whole and complete beings we once knew ourselves to be. Our missing parts are "out there" somewhere in the separation, and we must devote ourselves to finding them, suffering when we fail.

Authorizing our own reality, projecting our wishes onto reality, assigning meaning to the perceived world—all of this results from thinking with the mind of fear. This is the process, in the creating of a personality, by which we would make the separation real.

And this is the process by which we construct our world. Dividing up the Oneness into a kaleidoscope of variety, we perceive the many forms of our experience and then judge them along the lines of our fear. Let us get a feel for how this process occurs, to see the judging force at work in us, drawing the blueprints of reality.

## Drawing the Blueprints of Reality

Picture a series of dots:

```
•   •   •   •
•   •   •   •
•   •   •   •
•   •   •   •
```

These dots, in and of themselves, have no pattern of relationship. But now see them as four squares, each square composed of four dots. Notice how "real" and fixed this perception becomes! Now imagine four larger overlapping squares, each square composed of nine dots. We can make a cross, two columns, or any of an incredible variety of forms and patterns of relationship.

This is the act of judgment. By extracting forms out of the uniform field of Oneness, we give them meaning and order, judging them to be real. If we see two points of light blinking in sequence next to each other, we connect them as if a single point of light is "moving" in a particular direction. In seeing a relationship where none exists, we are imposing an illusion on top of reality.

Even our perception of up and down is arbitrary: People who wear goggles with lenses that invert the visual world "upside down" eventually learn to see the same world through these same goggles as "right side up." Those having psychedelic experiences have been known to see the visual field being created with their thoughts. With each step forward, there would be a band of emptiness on the horizon, the area in the visual field that had been hidden the step before. After a moment, this emptiness becomes filled in according to the thoughts and expectations of the perceiver, with an appropriate match of sensory data to complete the new picture!

Such perception is a learned phenomenon. We actively choose the perception we wish to have, and then see the results of our choice, thinking it to be an "objective reality." But in fact, our eyes and ears are receiving only what we have already decided they should receive, with the judgment already made before we see and hear them.

Helen Keller, until she learned to understand language, said that she really didn't exist in the strict sense of the word. Everything was a blackness through which she made her way, bumping into things, nothing having any meaning for her. But when Anne Sullivan drew the word "water" on the palm of her hand, simultaneously holding Helen's hand under a running faucet, the forces of perception gathered until the connection was made and she understood. In that moment, she said, the entire world revealed itself to her in a flash.

In the same way, certain aboriginal tribes that have never seen a photograph before are simply unable to see the patterns of meaning in the picture, meanings which would be obvious to us. Where we have learned to judge such patterns, they see a meaningless mass of dark and light patches. Similar stories are told of people who cannot make sense of two-dimensional drawings representing three-dimensional objects with which they are perfectly familiar. And kittens raised in a room with no vertical lines will bump into chair legs when taken out of the room because they have not learned to see them.

It is even said that the Aztecs were so vulnerable to the Spanish conquistadors because, never having had the experience of "ships floating on water," it was as if the Spaniards simply appeared out of nowhere on the shore. In more everyday terms, we notice that when we are thinking about buying a house, suddenly "For Sale" signs show up everywhere!

Adam and Eve in the Garden of Eden once again give us a metaphorical account of the origin of judgment. When Adam "named" everything in the Garden, he was, in fact, judging. He was giving meaning to it all and relating the meanings of each thing to every other. He was building a world of perception. Eating from the tree of the knowledge of good and evil brought the awareness of the differences upon which judgment depends. Before this, God called everything

"Good." Now, there would no longer be an equality among all things, no equal value being given to them all. Adam and Eve judge themselves "guilty" and hide from God. This judgment was the beginning of their suffering as they were "cast out" from the Garden, separated from their natural, heavenly state.

*Magic Eye,* the two-dimensional pictures that become three-dimensional, gives a wonderful demonstration of the judging process in motion. We are looking at what appears to be a jumbled mass of meaningless chaotic patterns, when suddenly the picture jumps out at us. Until this moment, we are fully confronted with our helplessness, unable to create order and meaning in the picture, unable to achieve the reality we wish. Rather than allowing things to be as they are, we activate our judging mechanism and "learn" to maneuver the eyes so as to find order out of the chaos. We give a "name" to the jumble of lines and dots. We set limits around certain parts, defining and circumscribing these parts as distinct from the rest. We pull out from the mass of confusion a set of lines that make up what we will call a "circle" here and a "triangle" there. We then relate these two to each other and build a world of meaning and relationship by the differences we see between them.

The Hindus describe the Oneness as an ocean, and the judging mind as that which tries to draw a circle around a "piece" of the ocean. The judging mind then declares everything inside the circle as different from the ocean. It accepts only what is inside as real. This is the world in which we live.

But inside the circle is still the same as outside—the circle does not, in fact, separate what is the same from what is the same. Nevertheless, we name it, judge it to be different, and insist on seeing it that way. In so doing, we deny the Oneness and take this illusion as the truth. Of course, this then has us feeling separate from and cut off from the rest of the ocean, our source. What's more, we're constantly in fear that we inside the circle will be swallowed up by the huge ocean outside the circle. So we build up our defenses to hold off the rest of the ocean, and hold on tightly to our view.

We do the same thing with each other. If I refuse to name you by my definitions, I will see you in your original state of perfection, and I would see myself in exactly the same way. There would be no more fear. Without fear, there would be no more separation, and no need for warring against each other. Because I *am* you, what's inside the circle is the same ocean as outside.

In *Magic Eye,* when we decide to see a particular shape and then construct that shape out of the uniform oneness, the picture gels and becomes concrete and we see the shape. It's the same when we judge, saying, for example, "That person wronged me." Suddenly he *becomes* a terrible person in our mind. We build up a whole story about him in our mind and see the evidence for justification everywhere. But then we find out he never said or meant what we thought, and suddenly the whole picture changes. That's how we create sickness. That's how we create insanity.

There was a poem found in the apron pocket of a 94-year-old woman who had just died in her room in a nursing home. It illustrates the point exquisitely:

### Nurse, look at me!

What do you see nurses, what do you see?
What are you thinking, when you're looking at me?

A crabby old woman, not very wise. Uncertain of habit with faraway eyes. Who dribbles her food and makes no reply when you say in a loud voice, "I do wish you'd try."

Who seems not to notice the things that you do, and forever is losing a stocking or shoe. Who's unresisting or lets not you do as you will. Is that what you're thinking, is that what you see? Then open your eyes, nurses, you're not looking at me.

I'll tell you who I am, as I sit here so still, as I do your bidding, as I eat at your will. I'm a small child of 10 with a father and mother, brothers and sisters who love one another.

A young girl of 16, with wings on her feet, dreaming that soon now a lover she'll meet.

A bride soon at 20, my heart gives a leap, remembering the vows that I promised to keep.

At 25 now, I have young of my own, who need me to build a secure, happy home.

A woman of 30, my young now growing fast, bound to each other with ties that should last.

At 40 my young sons have grown and are gone, but my man's beside me to see I don't mourn.

At 50 more babies play 'round my knee. Again, we know children, my loved one and me.

Dark days are upon me, my husband is dead. I look to the future, I shudder with dread. For my young are all rearing young of their own, and I think of the years and the love I have known.

I'm an old woman now and nature is cruel. 'Tis her jest to make old age look like a fool. The body, it crumbles, grace and vigor depart. There's now a stone where I once had a heart.

But inside this old carcass, a young girl still dwells, and now and again, my heart swells.

I remember the joy, I remember the pain, and I'm loving and living life over again.

I think of the years, all too few, gone too fast, and accept the stark fact that nothing can last.

So open your eyes, nurses, and see. Not a crabby old woman, look closer, see me.

## Getting Our Hands on the Controls of Perception: Bypassing the Chief Defense

With our feeling now for how thoughts create perception, we are ready for the "what to do about it." We have said that the task is to withdraw the perceptions we have projected upon reality, allowing things to be as they are. And this is precisely what we do when we find and face our fears, watching the fearful perceptions dissolve, no longer needing to make ourselves safe from imagined threat.

Facing fear is really a matter of bypassing the chief defense, for it is the chief defense which has us project these perceptions onto reality in the first place. In bypassing the chief defense, we do the opposite of what it has dictated, which may mean doing nothing at all, and thereby walk straight through our fear to watch it vanish. Without the intervening barrier of our defense, there is nothing to obscure reality-as-it-is.

At first, in bypassing the chief defense, the fearful thoughts it was protecting against may arise, tempting us to resurrect its barrier. But in finding and facing the fears at their source, we see again that they are not real. The wall that would stop us from this is understood as but smoke and mirrors, and we are free to walk straight through it unharmed.

To sum all this up, getting our hands on the controls of perception is a two-part process. First, we must withdraw our allegiance to the effects of perception. That is, we must stop believing that they are fixed and real, beyond our control, created by some external and absolute source. We must understand *how* we make them up, or at least consider *that* we make them up, and begin looking for the way to re-create them differently.

To recognize that we make up our perception is to recognize that the fear-defense strategy which has us make it up does not truly get us what we want. We no longer wish to impose our perception upon reality, thinking that it is the way to safety and to wholeness. We no longer look for external fulfillments, believing that the things of the world in and of themselves can make us happy. Instead, we look to the perceiver within, the one who makes up these things and assigns them arbitrary value.

The second part of the process is this: with our willingness to "see things differently," we also become willing to face the fear that motivated the perception. It is not enough simply to say, "I don't believe in my perception." We must be willing to act on this, bypassing the defense and facing the fear to prove it is unreal. It is not even necessary to actually face the fear, although this is often the only thing which will convince us. But in the moment we truly disbelieve our perception and become *willing* to act accordingly, its effects will disappear and the awareness of Truth will emerge spontaneously.

With the bypassing of our chief defense and the facing of our fear, our hands are on the dials of perception and *we now can choose* the world we would see. We tune the receiver to a new channel, the frequency of our essential nature, that which expresses our Joy.

In the doorway of the mind we understand that nothing of the world has the power to influence our Joy or our suffering; the choice is all determined from within. Not even a concentration camp, as Victor Frankl demonstrated in *Man's Search for Meaning,* can keep us from happiness when we master our thoughts and release our fear. Mother Teresa saw the opportunity to clean the manure off the sick and dying as the sweetest bliss—for her, she was cleaning and tending to her Beloved. A meal offered to someone who is starving is a welcome offer indeed. But a meal offered to someone undertaking a conscious fast is perceived quite differently. We must withdraw our attention from the value of things in the world as we have learned to perceive them, to what "inside" has us perceiving them the way we do. This gives us access to the levers and dials of Joy.

Healing occurs when we recognize that we have judged

reality as unjoyful, and then "forgive" the judgment. We can sit without deciding what reality "means" and let the original judgment of Oneness arise in our awareness. But to do this, we must be willing to bypass the chief defense that had us projecting the misperception to begin with.

For instance, we name ourselves unworthy, inadequate, "sinners." We build an entire picture of ourselves as bad and mistaken, wrong and guilty. And we can unname this, recognizing that we made the whole idea up. We then sit with that awareness, resisting the temptation of fear to defend with another perception. Instead, we wait for a deeper knowing, long buried under wraps of fear, to reveal our true Name.

Withdrawing our projections and letting go of judgments means fully comprehending that *nothing* in the world has an objective meaning beyond what we have given it. The "beginner's mind" of Zen is important here—we must constantly remember to practice "not already knowing" what a thing means. Indeed, if we could let go all pre-set assumptions about what things mean, and all of our automatic reactions to them, we would look upon the world as if for the first time. In that instant, its true and joyful nature would reveal itself, and our enlightenment would be complete.

The words "heal," "whole," and "holy" derive from the same root. When we see our wholeness and the wholeness of all things, we are seeing with holy perception and this automatically creates healing. We can heal everything in our body, mind, and soul by taking away the judgment that we were sick in the first place! No matter what meanings we have imposed upon ourselves, we are still, as in our original creation, perfectly whole, healthy, and complete. *Only our decision to see ourselves as sick had it seem to be so.* The key that opens the doorway of the mind is to let go of the meaning we have given to the situations of our lives, the meaning assigned by our core fear and chief defense. This is readily accomplished as we face the fear, doing the opposite of what our defense would have us do, and watch fear's perception dissolve.

Again, why would we resist this? Is it not good news? Only our struggle for control over reality has us stick defiantly to outmoded definitions and ways of being that cause us pain. Let us remember our commitment to release and to Joy. Let us invoke our passion for finding real Meaning underneath the stale assumptions of our unhappiness. For with this comes true Freedom and the recognition that we are not the victims of our world but its creators.

This step is so essential because it brings the power fully back into our hands. Enlightenment is not a matter of rearranging the objects of our perception, "redecorating our illusions," but getting at the source of perception and paving the way for an entirely new understanding. By doing this, we short-circuit fear's attempt to delay the confrontation with Truth, the Truth that *we* are responsible for our perception and only we can change it.

With this we can choose Joy at any moment, regardless of what seems to be happening "out there"; it is all made up in perception. No fear has a reality, a real power, to limit us in any way from making the choice for Joy. Here, at last, is the fulfillment we seek, the peace that cannot be imposed upon, the Joy that cannot be disturbed.

# EXERCISES

How do we build a perceptual world? We have said it starts with a thought. And thinking, it seems, is an automatic process that happens by itself. But in fact there is a "voice that precedes thought," that in us which chooses each and every thought we think. We willfully and intentionally "move" our consciousness in a particular way, choosing to activate a particular set of neurons, when we think a certain thought. You can actually feel this movement as a subtle shift of energy, a tweak of consciousness.

In choosing a particular thought, we begin to build the world of our perception. We then activate other thoughts to consolidate the picture, judging which ones will confirm and strengthen our view, to keep the picture from dissolving—we "hold the thought in mind." With this, we also push away other thoughts that are not part of the picture we are building, like sorting through files and isolating the particular file we wish. Again, you can feel this process and even see it reflected in the unique eye movement patterns that accompany particular thoughts.

Then there is a period where we secure our "thought picture," continually verifying to ourselves whether this is the picture we want. We cross-reference the thoughts with each other and check out their interactions to make sure they "work" the way we wish them to. Finally, we become so fixated on building and maintaining our picture that we lose sight entirely of the fact that we are generating these thoughts. We live "inside" the world we have created.

By this process, we attempt to make the separation real, building a perceptual world that "proves" we are separate. We select only those thoughts which create the perception of separation, forcing our attention into the tightly constricted range of what will further our goal, and exhaust ourselves in denying the rest.

This is the energy jam. We exert a tremendous energy in erecting the walls of our defenses to create a groove, a rut, within which we will allow the "right" thoughts to flow and refuse entry to the rest. We willfully force these thoughts into the channel of our making, the perception of our choice, defending against all else.

The effort involved in our vigil against Oneness, the repression of Truth, is enormous. This is literally the source of all strain and fatigue. The judgment of which thoughts will bring the reality we want and which ones must be banished depletes us thoroughly. Eventually, the fear of reality imposing itself upon our wishes wears us down mentally, breaks down the body, and deflates our spirit.

It is crucial, then, that we recognize this process and release the energy jam. We must turn our attention away from the results of perception and toward its source—the creator who is thinking it up! With this, we can see ourselves forcing energy into the groove and pushing away the rest, finally remembering that we are *choosing* to do this. The final step to freedom, where we choose instead to allow things to be as they are, becomes a simple matter of "stepping back" and not interfering. With this, we restore ourselves to our natural condition of health, fulfillment and Joy. The following exercises are devoted to just that.

## Exercise 1: Dissolving the Energy Jam— Asking "What Happens Next?"

In the exercise for finding our core fear, we asked, "What are you afraid will happen next?" Having found the core fear, we must now ask, "What actually does happen next?" in the interest of discovering that there is no threat.

Go back to your core fear. Visualize the picture of it in your mind. Get very specific and really bring it to life in your perception. Now write down the details of what is happening to you in that picture. Write in the present tense, as if it were happening now. For the rest of the exercise, your job is simply to stay with this narrative, repeatedly asking yourself the question, "What happens next?" and writing each answer as it comes to you.

Don't do anything to try to escape the fear; you want to go through it without employing your defense. Just ride out the story until it comes to a resolution of some sort. You are looking for a perception shift, where fear dissolves and you are free. You will feel the energy jam as your defense wants to assert itself and push away the fear. Stay with the process and you will naturally come to a point where the energy is released from its bindings, and a deep sense of relaxation, flow, and vitality is restored.

But we must arrive at this spontaneously; we do not want to shortchange ourselves when it comes to our Joy. Gently but firmly insist on staying with the fear, getting very specific with what you are experiencing each time you ask, "And what happens next?" Do not let yourself escape from the fear, not even by visualizing your death. (If death is the fear you must face, ask yourself "What happens next after I die," and see what it is like to be dead.) Wait, as patiently as necessary, for something to shift.

Eventually the fear passes, its consequences forgotten, as time moves on and the perception we were so invested in fades. We may have to go far into the future to see this—what do the things you are concerned about matter 100 years from now, when everyone you know and all that you have been striving for so earnestly is gone? But this is not cause for despair; only our fear would tell us this, and we must then see what happens next after the despair passes. Ultimately, it is the key to freedom and the release from the self-imposed prison of our perception.

When you have found the perception shift—and there is no mistaking it when you do—ask yourself, "What looks different now? What options do I see for dealing with my problems?" Or if these problems no longer exist, ask yourself, "What's possible for me now that didn't seem possible before? What am I free to do, who am I free to be?" Write down the answers to these questions as well, so that you may refer back to them as needed.

Let me relate here a particularly dramatic experience of someone working with this process. One night, an ICU nurse came to a group session I was holding. She was full of distress. She had just spent the day working with a terminally ill patient who should have died long before. This patient, however, continued to live in the most agonizing pain, day after day,

month after month. My patient, the nurse, had her own debilitating illnesses which were, at that time, possibly becoming
life-threatening. She had had a death wish for many years, but
had kept it under relative control . . . until now.

As she relayed her story to the group, visibly distraught by
the experience with her patient and the reminder of her own
situation, I helped her get in touch with her core fear. In a
few moments, she was writhing with discomfort, imagining
being trapped in the worst kind of pain, with no relief possible.
Repeatedly I said to her, with as much equanimity as I could
muster, "Stay with this image, remembering you are safe and
that you are simply going through an exercise to get free of
your fear. Let's see what happens next." She would describe
wave after wave of pain, pain which would not let go of her.
The entire group was caught up in their own fears, adding to
the intensity of charge in the air.

Several times, she wanted to escape the pain by imagining
that the "what happens next" was her death. Sensing that
this would leave her still vulnerable to the fear, not having
fully resolved it and seen it through to the other side, I asked
her to come back into her body just a little bit longer, and
get to know her fear all the way.

Again, she would describe the most agonizing scenes of
never-ending pain, screaming and writhing in her hospital
bed with no one coming to help her. Either they could not
hear her or they didn't care. In her visualization, she had
been abandoned by everyone, including God.

This went on for at least forty minutes. My only job was to
ask her over and over, "What happens next?" But she felt the
implicit support of the question, understanding that it was
meant as a guide to lead her out of fear. Courageously, she
stayed with it. I knew, in fact, that something in her wanted
to explore and understand this most fundamental part of
herself, and that there was a subtle satisfaction in touching so
deeply what had her running scared her entire life.

Finally, her agitation quieted down, her face and voice softened, and the aura of resentment she had always carried with her dissolved. Fully spent, she opened her eyes and said quietly to the group, "It's gone." In sharing her experience, she described how eventually the same old story she had been playing out her whole life got boring; it was old and stale and she wanted to move on. This was a remarkable statement coming from her—she had been fully immersed in the drama of her fear, not wanting to let it go, for fifty years! When someone asked her how she would deal with her real-life illness, she said, "I can see that, first of all, I was generating a lot of the problem with my constant worry and the tension that created, and second of all, the possibility of it doesn't scare me anymore—I know what it's like at its worst and I know that it eventually passes."

We have been stopped all our lives by a fear we have never really tested. With this exercise, we do test the fear and come to see it for what it truly is. We have lived through the experience of what actually would happen, not just some imagined horror, and discovered it is not what we had thought.

This is the true experience of insight, insight that shows the fear to be illusory and therefore frees us from fear's effects. To release the energy jam, we must get the insight that says no real threat is imminent. We may get insight, as well, into what gave rise to our core fear, to see that it is an arbitrary way of thinking based on earlier events. For instance, if we fear abandonment, feeling that our life is in danger if we are left, we may discover that the feeling that our life is in danger if we are abandoned comes from the thinking of the infant, whose survival did, in fact, depend upon not being abandoned. Really seeing this shows that we no longer depend on a caretaking adult for our survival. We stop jamming energy into the dead-end rut of thinking we have to defend against this fear, insisting reality look the way we want.

Knowing that all fears will pass, we want to practice asking ourselves "What happens next? What happens over time after the fear is gone?" We want to train ourselves to look to the other side of fear rather than stopping at the point of thinking how we can avoid it, a strategy which always leaves us in a state of fearful anticipation. We want to keep our sights set on the Joy of discovering that the ghosts which have been chasing us all our lives do not exist.

## Exercise 2: Embracing Fear, Releasing Resistance

This exercise borrows a technique from Vipassana (Insight) Buddhism to embrace the fear that otherwise makes us run. In so doing, the fear loses its meaning as something antagonistic, something fearful which must be defended against. Perception transforms as we see the fear to be "pure energy," withdrawing the meaning we had assigned to it.

Our practice involves bypassing the chief defense, doing the opposite of what it says to do. In the previous exercise, we also took action that was counter to what our defense prescribes, simply by staying with the fear rather than running from it. In this exercise, we more actively embrace the fear, going toward that which our defense would have us run away from.

There is a bumper sticker that says, *If God seems far away, guess who moved?* When we judge a thing and thereby separate from it, it takes on identity by virtue of the dividing line drawn between us and it. It now has a name; it is the something on the other side of the dividing line. It is something "out there," threatening to us by virtue of our not having control over it.

In running from our fear, deciding it is something that must be run from, we have been living in response to an arbitrary definition that we projected onto the world, and we have been suffering as a result. This meaning never was there. We are free. Free from the fear that says we can be happy only if we can control the world, making it conform to our wishes. Free from the need to judge this thing as "good" and that thing as "bad," having to find a way to force the "bad" to disappear from view. We are all pretending to be Atlas, trying to control a whole world of our making, having to bear its incredible weight upon our shoulders.

Knowing that we have made up all meanings and that we need not fear those things we thought meant "bad," we can release our tight hold on trying to control the world. There is no more need for striving and struggling to exhaustion for such a goal. There is no more need to fear that we'll never accomplish it. We can let go of our restlessness, freeing ourselves to discover something in us so much bigger than the little self we thought we were, so much bigger that we know we cannot be threatened. This is the true value of letting go of defenses, and never need we create the perception of threat or separation again.

In this exercise, we will discover these things by removing the judgment that has us separate from the things we fear, the parts of reality we would push away, and actively embrace them instead. If you wish, you may tape record this exercise in advance, allowing the necessary pauses to be recorded as well, so that you are free to fully concentrate on the practice without having to read as you go along.

Begin again by visualizing the scene of your core fear. With your eyes closed, imagine that you will be settling into this scene, staying with it for a long time, maybe forever. Each time your mind wants to run, to distract itself, to push away or change the scene somehow, bring it back to "just sitting" with the fear.

Explore the details of this scene. Again, bring it to life for yourself. You want to get to know that which has been having such an influence on who you are and how you perceive the world. What parts of the picture scare you the most? How do you try to relate to it to make yourself safer? How do you jockey for getting more of what you want?

Now, going into the part of this scene that scares you the most, concentrate on the physical sensations of your fear.

Notice the tangible feeling of fear as it lives in your body. This is a handle you can grab hold of to work with, something solid about the fear that you can relate to.

Begin to describe these sensations, keeping your attention on them, in the following ways: What shape does this sensation have? Draw the outline of it with your mind's eye and get very specific about the details. Bring it out in bold relief so that you see it with crystalline clarity.

Next, what weight does the sensation have? Imagine holding it in your hands and comparing it to different substances. Is it light and porous or dense and solid? Look at the variations in weight throughout its shape.

Next, what texture does it have? Is it smooth and shiny, rough and scratchy, spongy, cushiony or silky? Keep looking at the finer details of texture as you ask yourself these questions.

Finally, describe the movement of this sensation. Is it stuck or does it move in waves, does it pulse, throb, sting, or have tentacles that touch different points on the inside of your body?

In all of this, the practice is to actively go into the sensation, reversing the tendency to run from it, by exploring it fully and getting to know its tiniest details. As if looking at the sensation under a microscope, you want to open up the doors of it and actively invite it in, letting it get closer and closer a bit at a time.

Remind yourself frequently that it's okay for the sensation to be just the way it is. It doesn't have to go away. You want to settle into being with it, releasing the thought that says you must do something about it. Let it just float there, giving it lots of room to be. It's okay for it to float quietly; it doesn't have to go away. Soften the tight grip you have held around it, letting yourself loosen, open, relax around it.

Now, open up the space around it twice as much. Take a deep breath and give it lots of breathing room.

And now, let the bottom drop out as you open up the space inside all the way. The sensation now floats in infinite vastness, just floating quietly, a tiny sensation in the universe within. You can choose to place your attention on it or anywhere you please in this internal cosmos. The sensation doesn't force you to attend to it at all. You are free to if you choose. You are also free to choose a new perception.

In this exercise, we stop trying to make that which we fear "go away." We reverse the meaning we gave to it when we judged it as "bad." We can feel ourselves assigning this meaning as we catch ourselves trying to push it away, judging it as something that "should not be here." This is how we would force reality to conform to our wishes, resisting reality-as-it-is, and separating from our oneness with them accordingly. We want to practice embracing all things exactly as they are, stripping away our assigned meanings and letting them register on our consciousness in their true state.

Fear or pain, for example, can be understood as neutral sensations, the raw experience of energy. They can even be understood as demonstrating our ability to feel deeply, a testimony to the miracle of being alive. They can give a rich and profound, bare-bones contact with Existence, our interaction with the Mystery of it all, no numbing of awareness to keep us from touching the Power of who we really are.

## Exercise 3: Connecting with the Choicemaker (Meta-thinking)

"Connecting with the choicemaker" is a most powerful technique for not only embracing but actively choosing reality-as-it-is. It is based on the understanding that reality-as-it-is is already perfect and complete. Any perception of "something needing to be fixed," any wish or attempt to change things, even the striving to fulfill our dreams of arranging circumstances to our liking—all these are built on the fear that says something is wrong with things-as-they-are, something threatens us with our core fear. Our constant efforts to fix and change then become the way our chief defense is exercised.

When we surrender our chief defense and face the fear underneath, we see that reality-as-it-is is indeed perfect and complete, with all its change and flux, apparent limitation and loss. Our task, therefore, is to let go the resistance to this and actively choose for it to be the way it is.

It is a spiritual truism that everything that seems to happen to us (in our perception) is the result of what we have asked for. In this exercise, we will come to the direct experience of this by acknowledging that we have, in fact, chosen that all things be just the way they are, instead of seeing them as needing to be denied, changed, or somehow erased from existence. We will catch ourselves in the act of judging reality and thereby giving it the definitions and names that bring it to life. We name reality and we name ourselves as separate individuals. We, therefore, want to realize that we are the ones who name, not the thing named; the ones who choose, moment-to-moment, not the choice already made and fixed.

This practice is actually devoted to transforming those experiences which we have chosen and which we do not like. Again, it will seem that we have not chosen them at all. The way to transform them is to acknowledge that we *have* chosen them, we wanted to experience them for some reason, *and then to choose them consciously.* That is, we look for a reason that we might have wanted to experience them, and then intentionally continue choosing to experience them for this purpose. We thereby release the resistance against our choice and are free either to continue choosing it or not.

Whatever your reason, come up with some value, purpose, or goal that your experience of the moment is helping you accomplish. Whether it is to give you the experience that you may get tired of it and eventually dispense with it, or to teach you the lessons of life, or simply to give the chance to feel what it is like to be alive, exploring life in all of its variety, find a way to give it a value that lets you tap into the feeling of having chosen it.

We want to practice choosing our experiences intentionally, not choosing them in secret and then building up a resistance to them. For this only serves to keep us locked into the ancient and tired game of trying to change reality-as-it-is, where we end up instead locking ourselves more deeply into our suffering. We must turn around to face the fear behind this defensive strategy, and choose, embrace, even love the experience we are having.

Begin, then, by saying or writing, "I choose this experience of _____," and fill in the blank with whatever you are experiencing, thinking, or feeling at the moment. Exclude nothing or you will harbor the belief that some things are automatically given and are therefore not available for your transformation. Simply make a moment-to-moment accounting of what is in your awareness, saying "I choose this experience of _____ in this moment," remembering your possible reason(s) for choosing it. Other words are helpful for keeping your perspective fresh, such as "I want this experience of _____," "I'm creating this experience of _____," or "I'm making up this experience of _____."

After saying or writing out each of these sentences, you may well feel that you are still a passive recipient of the experience and not the creator of it. To this, you will want to say or write something to the effect of, "Here I am choosing to have this experience of not being the creator of my experience." The point is to actively acknowledge that everything in your awareness is, on some level, your choice.

In seeing that we choose our experience, we realize that we may create it differently. Not that we need to any longer, just that we are free to. For in seeing that we create it all, we automatically change (our perception of) it by taking away the resistance to it. It was the resistance that actually preserved it in frozen form, keeping us from recognizing we are not victimized by it, at its mercy. We are instead its creator, capable of creating it differently, but only after embracing it in its present form, the form we chose, we created, we wished into existence.

Our resistance to reality-as-it-is is, itself, part of reality-as-it-is, and we can *choose* our resistance in order to see its perfection. This is releasing the resistance to our resistance. When we have resistance to the idea that we choose the reality we are experiencing, we create a resistance that becomes a part of reality-as-it-is.

To practice with this, we will use a process I call "meta-thinking." In meta-thinking, we work on *choosing* that which represents our resistance to this practice, such as "I'm choosing the experience that this practice isn't working; I'm choosing the thought that I don't know how to do this; I'm choosing to be distracted; I'm choosing to numb out," and so on.

Other such meta-thoughts include the following: "I say I want to experience the thought that I'm forgetting, that I'm getting cloudy, that I'm stuck, etc., and I experience it. And I choose the experience that has me thinking I'm not choosing to forget, to be cloudy, to be stuck, etc., but that it is happening to me without my control." Meta-thinking is becoming aware of all the thoughts we have about our thoughts or thought processes.

In "connecting with the choicemaker" and "meta-thinking," we realize that absolutely nothing has the power to keep us from Freedom, for we create all such ideas of limitation. We create them all! When we choose to have things be just as they are, suddenly they are illuminated as perfect expressions of reality-as-it-is and therefore the Joy we seek. They are no longer that which is to be resisted; they are our very answer. We realize we have created the resistance. And with this awareness, we can know ourselves as the choicemaker that can also choose differently.

Once we have developed some skill in this and are really getting a sense of freedom and mastery over our creations, we want to include in our meta-thinking the awareness that we are choosing to end the session, leaving the experience wherein we see that we are choosing it all. Practice with the awareness of why we would choose this to go back to our "usual" state of (un)awareness, of why we would ever move back into the perception that it was just an exercise and not an experience of truer perception. Work with the thought that says "end the session," and know that you are choosing it. Then consider choosing to stay in the experience forever! On our final return to Joy, we will never again think the thoughts which satisfy separation, but will give ourselves fully to Truth. We will give up the world of fear's perception completely and forever, choosing to let go all old ideas of a separate self, moving permanently into the experience of Oneness and Joy.

The following are some samples of "connecting with the choicemaker" and "meta-thinking." The idea of energy in the second sample could be substituted with anything else we feel blocked to, such as remembering we are safe if we feel scared, remembering we are free if we feel trapped, remembering our Joy if we feel sad, and so forth.

### Sample 1

I am choosing the heaviness I'm experiencing. I am creating this tension, the feeling that this is hard work. I choose to see the light coming through the way it is, and I want this feeling of separation from the objects I see around me. I am creating this worry I have about the day, the worry that I must get somewhere on time, etc. I'm choosing now to realize that all this is me. I choose to realize *everything* is me, everything is consciousness, one with my consciousness. I'm choosing to be in my head, not realizing this. I'm choosing to be numb, to not know what is going on. Everything that's happening is exactly what I chose and wanted, even the thought that says this isn't true. I wanted this thought because I'm the creator

of my universe wanting to know what it is like to think I'm
not the creator of my universe. I'm the All tapping into the
experience, that is part of my Allness, that says I'm not the
All, but rather I'm a little mind stuck in this body and this
little experience where things seem to happen to me. Yes,
here I am wanting to have this experience and then having
it! It's perfect, beautiful, how wonderful—I'm really having
the experience of it, complete with the thought that this isn't
working. I, the creator of it All, am choosing, creating; I am
the only creator, manifesting the creation out of the Void,
and this experience I'm having is the very experience I wanted
to create. It is all as I have chosen; it is all my breath poured
out into form; it is all my heart and my love molding, nurturing,
and breathing life into Existence. I am! I breathe! I love, and
all is. I am a creator and I am free! What delightful forms and
thought-forms (with all their feelings, senses, mental shapes,
and colors) I play with as I think and have new experiences
of creation with each thought and the feelings, perceptions
(no, they are universes!) that come with the thought. I am!

## Sample 2

I am choosing this experience of having no energy. I want
to be tired and so I am having this experience. I feel the wall
of smoke I have created, keeping me from feeling energetic,
keeping me isolated from energy. I love this wall of smoke,
thick, seemingly impenetrable smoke that has me feeling
"tucked in," away from what's on the other side of it. I feel
the anxiety I create with the thought that I have to stay away
from the other side. I choose and love this anxiety—this is
going into the wall of smoke with the potential of going
through. I love this anxiety, I choose it; it tingles, it courses
through my veins as pure Aliveness, the life force, my very
essence. And now I choose to go through the wall to the other
side, into the clear and free Light! I look back and see the
wall of smoke and what was on the other side (me—huddled

away in the dark) as all part of this Light, Consciousness, taking different forms. And with this Light, there is nothing but Energy all around (and in). The Light *is* Energy, and it has always been my experience. I just need to tap into this understanding, feeling the release and Freedom, not thinking that the experience back on the other side of the wall is all I can let my mind pay attention to (where I therefore can't feel the energy) and then see how the energy of Freedom and Peace and Light want to be translated in each situation.

A friend of mine, in working with this kind of process, told the story of how he had a broken toe. It was so sensitive even the bedsheets resting on it caused him pain. Then he remembered himself and practiced choosing his experience. Letting go of the attachment to a thought of "this is real," he began transforming his perception of the "painful" toe into something he chose for his growth and the powerful sensation of being able to feel so exquisitely. After a while, without quite noticing when, he realized the pain had completely disappeared. He got out of bed and put some weight upon it. No pain whatsoever. He began jumping up and down on it. Still no pain. He went outside. As he was about to cross the street, he had a fearful thought: "What if my toe should become painful as I am crossing the street and I cannot make it to the other side safely?" As he put his foot on the ground with his next step, the pain pierced through him with all sharpness. Realizing what had happened, he corrected his thought. With the next step, the pain was gone. He made a game of this play of perception as he continued walking across the street, one step painful, the next step pain-free, the next painful, the next pain-free, as he shifted his perception back and forth.

There is a movement, especially in the United States, of firewalking workshops. In these seminars, people gather for perhaps as little as four hours to learn how to walk on burning coals. The "how to" of it is simple: With the expectation that we will be able to walk on fire, and the witnessing of the group leader being able to do it, suddenly we tap in to the part of us which knows we are choosing our entire experience and can literally re-create the definition of fire as something that does not have to burn.

The preparation in these workshops involves nothing more than visualizations, dealing with fears and the generation of excitement over the possibility. There is no more "secret" than that. Suddenly, everyone is able to defy the "facts" of reality, and what was previously cause for great fear can become a thing of great Joy and Freedom. My personal experience was that a tremendous energy opened in my center that poured out and surrounded my body in the shape of a bubble that went under my feet as well. Walking across the coals, I was in an ecstatic state, and the burning embers felt like butterfly wings tickling the bottoms of my feet. There was no evidence of burning and I felt no pain.

The biblical phrase "the Kingdom of God" may be best understood as an allegorical reference to the "kingdom" within, the kingdom of our minds. The "keys" to this kingdom are nothing other than that which opens up the mind to its true state. Let us assume our rightful place as rulers of this kingdom by recognizing that we choose every thought and experience. We have chosen the thoughts and experiences that seemed to have us separate from Oneness. In knowing this, we cannot fool ourselves into thinking we are caught in the experience of separation. Rather, we remember that even this thought of separation is something we have chosen and created, all from within the perfection of the Oneness we have never left.

# CHAPTER 5

# THE DOORWAY OF THE BODY

Even your body knows its heritage and its rightful
need and will not be deceived. / And your body is
the harp of your soul, / And it is yours to bring forth
sweet music from it or confused sounds.
                                   —Kahlil Gibran, *The Prophet*

Roger, a 46-year-old electrician, came into my office one day
in excruciating pain. His doctors had diagnosed a pinched
nerve in his back. He could not sit up, nor could he lie down;
he began the session sitting half-propped on his elbow with
many pillows. I asked him when all this began and he said,
"The other day, right after our last session." Subtle hint! I
reviewed the session with him and sensed that he had some
repressed feelings around a conversation we had had about
his desire to go back to school to advance his career. When
I asked him what these feelings might be about, he gave me
a blank stare. Perhaps it had been a false lead. I decided to
try some hypnosis with him.

It was difficult getting past the distraction of his pain, but
soon we were in a hypnotic state. Asking him to free-associate,
while under hypnosis, to any impressions that emerged relative

to his back, he immediately flashed on a mental picture of a red book. I waited to see if anything would spontaneously follow. It didn't. I asked him if, at any time in the past, he had had difficulty with his back. Then the whole thing unraveled . . .

He began welling up with tears as he recalled a time when he was newly married. He wanted to go back to school to be able to earn a better living for his wife. She, however, became very upset with him for this, fearing it would take him away from her. He was torn between his desire to go back to school and his love for her. When she would not yield and the turmoil became too great for him, he found himself leaning over to pick up one of his schoolbooks (red), and at that moment, his back went out. This kept him from being able to start the semester on time. He never did go to school.

The entire episode had been completely repressed in his awareness until this time. Now it was pouring out, after years of being pent up in his back. He was crying buckets about his anger at his wife for being selfish and simultaneously his great love for her. As he cried, his body began to contort, twisting and turning, almost writhing with emotion. At the end of the outburst, all was quiet. Spontaneously, he opened his eyes from the hypnosis and whispered with amazement, "My back doesn't hurt anymore!" There was not a trace of pain. A checkup with his physician confirmed that there was no evidence of a pinched nerve.

Fear is not simply a mental affair. The thoughts of fear are translated in the body in a variety of ways. Each subtlest thought of fear has its corresponding physical response. This is the mind's projection of thought into that which we can perceive. In the body, this manifests as physical/emotional "blockages"—constrictions in blood flow, breath, energy, and self-expression. Tension, pain, illness, aging, and death are the visible and tangible representations of fear at work. Or more precisely, they are the representations of our chief defense at work, as it responds to the core fear with its strategy of "resistance against" the fear, bracing and tensing to fight it off.

When the noise of our fear makes it too difficult to hear and work with our thoughts, it is strategic to discharge the physical energy of the fear from our bodies first, undoing fear's projection, making it possible to quiet down enough to do the work of transforming ourselves.


## Contacting the Bodymind

We have said that each thought of fear has its corresponding response in our body, as the chief defense maneuvers to protect us physically from the fear. Remember, we have taken the body to be that which defines us as a separate self, and so we must protect it if we are to protect our separation. But exactly how do these fears and defenses, mechanisms of the mind, translate into the body?

The physical body is the separating entity *par excellence,* for it is the playground of so many of our definitions of ourself and of our responses to the world. That is, we play out the ideas about who we are and how we respond to the world, onto the body. It is a living record of our assumed ideas about who we are and what reality is. Therefore, it is possible to change these assumptions and ideas to re-create the body and affect its processes.

The body seems to define us (gives visible and tangible expression to the idea of us) as very tiny in space and completely bound in time, in the face of an infinitely huge universe full of surprises and threats over which we have little control. Therefore, we feel obliged to spend our time attempting to build such control as defense against these threats. Thus is born what the Buddhists call "the body of fear."

The way out, as always, involves facing our fear. When we take physical actions against our fear, we put our body—a projection of our thoughts—into the body of the world—

also a projection of our thoughts—in order to play out the projections and face our fear, discovering it does not come to pass. In the doorway of the mind, we did this in a purer fashion, withdrawing our projections. In the doorway of the body, we work directly with the projections as they seem to be happening "out there," separate from mind, in the world of our dreaming.

## Releasing the Energy Jam Through the Doorway of the Body

When we project our fear thoughts into physical form, we literally shape our body and our perception of other bodies. In deciding that the way to stay safe from our core fear is to exercise our chief defense, we are attempting to create the reality we wish, a reality where the fear is no longer hanging over us. But this effort has us, as we have said, seeing the signs of fear everywhere, that we may be prepared to fend off the threat with our chief defense. And this hypervigilance has us assume and perceive threat where it does not exist. We, therefore, respond with defensiveness when there is no need. It is this fact that leads to the energy jam.

In Chapter 4 we talked about the energy jam, where we force our thoughts into a dead-end rut as we insist on defining things according to the prescripts of our fear/defense strategy. When reality tells us that our definition is incorrect, rather than accepting this new information, we insist on seeing things our way. To do this, we create a narrow rut into which we jam our thoughts, forcibly pushing away all other thoughts. This rut cannot go anywhere, for reality will not "pick it up," and so we try to freeze reality until we can get it to comply.

We know this experience in ourselves when we say, "I'm thinking so hard my head hurts." This forcible and willful pushing away of all contrary thoughts, a sort of "freezing up" against reality, has its physical aspect, usually experienced first in the diaphragm. We brace ourselves against reality-as-it-is by holding our breath, as if this would stop time. We then tense various other parts of our body—our shoulders, shrugged to encase and protect our hearts; our faces, to search more vigorously for the signs that will confirm the reality we wish; our backs, curling over to protect our stomachs and other "vital organs." Ultimately, we move the whole body in the direction of either fight or flight. We refuse to address reality-as-it-is and either take aggressive action against its threat or retreat into isolation, strategizing new ways to accomplish our goal.

We further develop a variety of lifestyle responses involving the body: We tense our muscles in chronic patterns; we furrow our foreheads, focusing the eyes to enhance our worrying fixation on the problem; we become overweight for comfort and protection; we build up our physical strength to fight against reality and feel powerful over the forces of fear; we give in to our weakness and neglect the body; we employ facial expressions and bodily gestures designed to evoke certain responses from others, that they will leave us alone or protect and take care of us; and an endless dance of other gestures.

Ultimately, all of these manifest as "blockages," "emotional cysts" of various sorts that interrupt the free, healthy, and natural flow of things. That is, when we resist the flow of reality-as-it-is, we create a blockage to that flow. Arteriosclerosis or hardening of the arteries is such a resistance, as is asthma, hypertension, sexual dysfunction, migraine headaches, and blood clots. The fear that is manifesting as these blockages—constricting our flow of energy, blood, breath, and self-expression—must be discharged from the body if our transformation is to be complete. If the genesis of sickness is in the fears we project onto the body, then its healing comes from the dissolution of these fears, first mentally, then, in a spontaneous cause-effect way, physically. Physical health, then, becomes a natural result of joyous living.

It is now being discovered that the physical blockages created by fear are not just in the muscles but also in the fascia (the connective tissue), meninges (the membranes enclosing the brain and spinal cord), and even the tendons. Several wonderful new instruments and therapeutic modalities— Rolfing, Bioenergetics, the "somato-emotional release" of Cranio-sacral therapy, and others—are now on the scene and can help release these blockages to effect physical, psychological, and spiritual healing. In these techniques, various physical maneuvers are applied to free the bound-up energy, so that it may move through the blockages and restore healthy functioning. In certain types of Gestalt and other psychotherapies, the bound energy is expressed with the beating and pounding of pillows, accompanied by the full expression of any sound that wants to come forth. The patient emerges with a look of having been "cleansed," as if the energy field, darkened by the fear of restriction, is now freshly scrubbed and shining.

## The Urge to Express

This is really but a facilitating or catalyzing of a natural biological mechanism (though that, too, is determined by our assigned definitions). Our human organism wants to *express* (as opposed to the suppression, repression, and depression of blocked energy), *externalize*, even *expel* what was bound up within. For example, the sneezing, coughing, and vomiting reflexes move harmful matter outside the body. But so, too, with our innate urge to express the spirit, where the energy bound up in the diaphragm (affecting the lungs and breathing patterns as well) naturally presses forth to make sounds of all sorts—shouting for joy, screaming from fear, groaning, yelling, and so on. And in the supreme act of physical expression, the male body expels its semen, and the female body utters forth its soul's reflection in the birth of a child.

Again, all of this attests to the natural mechanism of the bodymind's attempt to *express* itself "outwardly" into a projected space and time. The following case history illustrates the point.

## Tracy

Tracy was a 29-year-old woman who took a workshop that put her in touch with her core fear and chief defense. The session was full of meaning for her and she seemed to move through to a successful conclusion. But when it came time to create the "mandala," drawing one's experience within a circle on a piece of paper with crayons, she found her hands went into extreme tetany. With a crayon clenched in her contorted hand, the muscles of her forearm extraordinarily tense and rigid, she began investing all of herself in making the crayon move upon the paper. Her face was twisted with the effort, her forehead furrowed, and like a Zen student attempting to solve a koan (a paradox), her full self was poured into the project. However, she could not get the crayon to move on the paper.

While all the other participants had completed the session and gone home for the night, she remained, still bound and determined to succeed with her drawing.

In the morning when the other participants returned, they found the floor of the workshop room strewn with beautiful drawings, Tracy still assiduously at work creating more. Her face was completely transformed, no longer tense and strained but glowing with the radiance of a spirit released. After a while, she had spent herself and felt complete.

She looked up and told the room that she had relived a time when she was five years old and was drawing with her crayons. Her parents came into the room, and recognizing her talent, gave her a subtle message of disapproval. They feared that she would grow up to become an artist, and wanted her to have a more "practical" career. Sensing their fear and disapproval, Tracy froze the incident, with all the accompanying emotions, in the muscles of her forearm and hand, as if to lock herself up so that she would not upset her parents when the impulse to draw grew strong again. The beautiful drawings which now covered the workshop floor were a deep expression of her spirit which, until this working through, had been locked up in the muscles of her arm and hand.

In the doorway of the body, then, we employ a variety of techniques to release the physical energy that has been bound up by fear. We have been using the body in set ways that inform and are informed by our personality, chronic patterns of bracing against our core fear. We have adopted a certain stance toward reality, either resisting it or allowing it when it does not threaten. In either case, fear is the director of our "body language," and we must either move the body against our fear or stand quietly without responding at all. Breaking up the rigid patterns of personality-expressed-through-the-body, we move through our resistances by giving up our automatic, physical reactions to fear. This releases huge reserves of energy, spontaneity, and creativity, the physical representatives of Joy. We become free to express a great variety of aspects of ourselves, re-creating ourselves entirely if we wish.

Moving the body in these ways bypasses the chief defense as it has been playing out in a physical way through habitual patterns of tensing, bracing, constricting, and withholding. The doorway to Joy through the body is flung open as we break through or gently release such blockages and sing the song of our spirit.

## EXERCISES

If what we perceive is driven by the thoughts we choose, and the thoughts we choose are driven by our core fear, then what we perceive is the symbolic representation of our core fear. We might say that what we perceive is a communication, in symbolic form, of what our fear is saying. Therefore, if we learn to decipher the code of such communication, it can tell us how the core fear is playing out in our lives. This gives the necessary awareness that we may act to release our fear and watch our perception change accordingly.

So it is when the object of our perception is the body and the ways in which personality is expressed through the body. Our gestures and actions, pain and illness all communicate how the core fear is being manifested physically. Listening to their messages, learning the lessons they have to teach, we may transform our relationship to them as we find and face the fear. The greater our release from fear, the more these communications are replaced by expressions of Joy.

Therefore, we want to explore how we are using our bodies in response to the core fear. We want to explore how we are acting out our chief defense, what we are physically doing to try to protect ourselves from the fear.

Perhaps we are responding to an experience of loss that came early in life, so that our chief defense involves holding on to what we can. This response may make us unwilling to let go when necessary, to be able to flow with the changes of life. Such a holding pattern can manifest in the intestines when, as children, we learn to hold in our eliminations, afraid of the experience of relaxing and letting go, unable to trust the natural rhythms of growth and change, birth and death, gain and loss. Physically, this can lead to constipation, irritable bowel, or other expressions of tension in those areas of the body involved in holding on.

If we are exposed to a fear that has us repeatedly "catching our breath," we might develop a personality style that reflects this pattern, continually anticipating the next surprise, our breathing rapid and shallow, our muscles readied for flight. We may become hypervigilant, eyebrows raised and adrenaline high, always cautious, anxious, afraid. Symptomatically, we may develop asthma as the expression of an anxiety that is ever ready to "take our breath away," or chronic fatigue as our adrenal glands become exhausted.

Posture and "body language" also communicate our defensive response to fear. If we are afraid of being punched in the stomach, literally or figuratively, we might walk around with our shoulders hunched over, caving in the stomach, to protect ourselves. This maneuver constricts our breathing, as the chest is no longer free to fully expand and the diaphragm is tensed. Such constriction puts undue strain on the organs held in the stomach and the digestive juices churn in response to an acidic or bitter experience of life.

Whether or not one is able to decipher the code of the physical expression of their emotional-mental experience, we can work with the body to undo the effects of fear being played out upon it. Again, this is a matter of physically facing our fear, moving our body in ways the fear says not to, expressing aspects of who we are that fear has had us suppress, and releasing the pressure built up behind the walls of fear manifesting in physical form. This is how we heal through the doorway of the body.

Regardless of whether we achieve such healing through the doorway of the body, mind, or spirit, all three relax into their rightful place and harmonious functioning when any one is released. As pertains to the body, finding and facing fear will enhance physical health, expand our repertoire of expression through the body, and dissolve the messengers of fear in our perception. The body then becomes a marvelous vehicle for the expression of our Joy and Purpose.

## Exercise 1: Revealing Private Thoughts

In Buddhist philosophy, the mind is considered a sixth sense. Just as our body's five senses create effects that we perceive as the phenomenal world, so does the mind create such effects. Indeed, our mental interpretation of the sense impressions given by the eyes, ears, nose, body, and tongue are all we really know of the world. Therefore, our thoughts are as powerful as our actions, if not more so. To think about hitting someone has the same effects on us as does commiting the act itself. Our thoughts, we might say, are actions that have not yet become physical.

This is where the idea of private thoughts comes in. When we believe we can keep certain thoughts private, we fool ourselves into believing that our thoughts do not have real effects. As long as no one knows about them (through our telling them), we imagine they remain invisible. Of course, the tension, guilt, fear, and defensiveness that this creates in us, all of which may be readily picked up by others, is the real concern, and believing otherwise simply keeps us powerless to change our experience.

Sharing private thoughts, then, is a way to stop harming ourselves, and to discover that we no longer need to carry such tension and defensiveness. We discover as well that we are responsible for what we create with our thoughts and can actively, through sharing private thoughts, create with intention. In the doorway of the body, we bring the "nonphysical" actions of our thoughts into the physical arena by sharing them. We face our fears by giving physical expression to that which we believed should be kept hidden, and watch the fear dissolve as no catastrophe results.

Let's explore how this works. We use the body as the ultimate "proof" that we have separated from Oneness. For it seems to fence off a little part of the one Mind and says that everything within the fence is "me" and everything else is not. This is the essence of our declaration of separation. And if thinking the thoughts of separation is a defense whose purpose is to keep out the awareness of reality-as-it-is, then the body becomes the agent for this goal. It will "contain" these thoughts within its shell, keeping away the truth "outside."

We developed the idea of private thoughts as proof that who we are is not of Joy. There must be something shameful and guilty about us if we are constrained to keep certain aspects of who we are private and hidden behind the secret walls of the body.

Again, like Adam and Eve in the Garden of Eden, we have eaten of the forbidden fruit and must hide this fact from God and others. We cover up our shame, now projected onto the body's nakedness. Ultimately we feel so guilty that we must be cast out of our original Home, separated from the Joy we once knew.

All of this is undone, as before, by confronting the fear that motivates it. As long as we would protect and hide certain thoughts, we give ourselves evidence, never tested, that there must be something too risky to share. Exposing our private thoughts, taking off their cover, is a way to disprove the idea that we are separate and hidden inside the body, that who we are is shameful and must be kept secret. Indeed, holding private thoughts creates a cascade of fantasies which, once spoken, gets measured against reality-as-it-is and takes on an entirely new, compassionate aspect.

In the doorway of the body, we use the power that we have assigned to the body to break down the very barriers that it erected. If it erected these barriers by keeping certain thoughts hidden, then we want to move past these barriers, facing our fear, by letting such thoughts be known. We can speak the thoughts that we have been keeping private, thereby making them physical, projecting "out there" what we believed was locked up "in here."

To express our private thoughts is to dissolve the walls of separation that seemed to be imposed between minds by bodies. It is to glimpse the Oneness and to know Joy. Fear dissolves as we discover that no terrible consequences occur when we reveal our private thoughts, doing that which we were afraid of. We are free to be ourselves and let reality be as it is.

In her book *Mutant Message*, Marlo Morgan tells of a tribe of Australian aborigines who appeared uncannily psychic. While moving along in a particular direction, for example, without anyone speaking a word, all sixty or so changed direction in the same way and at the same time. She inquired how this was possible. One of them told her that, because they have no secrets from each other and tell no lies, they do not have to erect the mental barriers that would keep their thoughts hidden from each other. Here is the one Mind in action!

This practice holds the key to total Freedom—no hiding, no tension, no worry about whether or not you are "good enough" or accepted. The simple act of revealing private thoughts, breaking down the walls of shame, can remove everything that has stood in the way of Joy. And the access is completely within your power. Just say the words and, even if you are not accepted for what is said, find that you have made *yourself* free, discovering you can come out of hiding and live the life you want.

Here is the exercise: Find someone with whom you feel safe and who agrees to be the listener. Reveal to that person as many thoughts about yourself as you are able and ready to share, thoughts that you have feared would bring rejection, disapproval, or abandonment. Tell how you have tried to create a certain impression, to have people see you in a certain light, by keeping some aspects of yourself suppressed while emphasizing others. Say also that you are doing this to set yourself free from too many years of fear and suffering. Invite support and reassurance that you will be accepted for who you are.

As you advance in your practice, take on some of the more "intense" or "real" fears that need to be shared. Tell how you have been living from your core fear, how afraid you are, how guilty or ashamed you feel, and how you distort, defend, or manipulate so others will see you in a certain way that you think will get you what you want. Blow the cover off your disguise by revealing it as much as you are able without incurring too much fear. This is the true meaning of forgiveness: forgiving or letting go of *your* illusions about yourself and the need to distort yourself to get love.

In the end, you will want to say everything, every fear that comes up, everything you want to hide, so that you may not be held captive any longer. Practice over and over until you find the courage and honesty to reveal it all, to face all fear, to risk everything. Remember your absolute commitment not to suffer, not to be lost anymore. Above all else, you want to discover you are safe and you can relax in life. You want to be free to be your true Self.

At this point, your fear may be asking, "What if the person I share my thoughts with abuses the information?" Properly understood, the focus will be more about the freedom *we* experience when we come out the other side of our fear, so that even if we should be rejected, our perception of who we are is transformed. The rejection is understood as the other person's fear and not a true message about ourselves. For in our freedom from fear, there is no defensive need to perceive ourselves as rejectable, knowing that we are safe and whole. Our attention then is drawn to the other person's suffering, for in their rejection, they deprive themselves of the freedom we are experiencing.

The ultimate answer, however, is this: Once we have become willing to share all of our private thoughts, we are in the experience of Oneness. We see that the other person is literally one with us, the same as us, and there is nothing to hide from them. We know that who we are is perfectly acceptable and worthy, and we see that the same is true for them. At that point, what they get from our communication, regardless of the words we use, is the Joy of our Freedom. The other person, in their oneness with us, literally experiences the same Freedom. They cannot help but experience what we are experiencing.

This is the perception of others that leads to healing. Only when we see ourselves as sick (physically or emotionally) do we see others that way, and seeing others that way locks us into the perception of a world where such sickness seems real. We see ourselves in that world and therefore take on the perception. But seeing the other as perfectly healed frees both of us, for we stand in the perception where sickness—the evidence that we are separate from our wholeness—is understood to be impossible.

It is necessary, however, that we take measured steps to reach this point, facing our fear in "divided doses." As always, we must be wise in our choices. We don't want to rush in to share something which might generate too much fear and damage the trust we are building. Eventually, all must be shared if we are to be truly free. But in the interest of getting to this freedom as quickly and effectively as possible, we want to be strategic in our approach.

So make sure you begin your practice with someone whom you know is safe. Again, we'll come to the point where we will no longer need this limit, because the fear that they might abuse the information or share it with others won't own us. For now, however, find someone whom you know, intellectually, if not emotionally, will accept you. You will still be facing your fear, which runs on a different engine from intellect and will try to convince you every which way it is not safe. But you don't want to add fear to fear should the other person give you "evidence" (really, a perception of your own making) that it is not safe to share your private thoughts.

## Exercise 2: Variations on the Theme—Eye Contact, Mirror Work, and "Reparenting"

Other ways to reveal your private thoughts include the following: Make eye contact with someone, moving closely into each other's space, and hold your gaze until you completely relax. Let yourself be fully seen, exposed, as you resist the temptation to hide yourself in some way. Become aware of the things you do with your face and body to keep the other person from seeing who you really are. What do you do to avoid having them see your insecurity, your love, your shame, your hope, your despair? What do you do to have them see you as intelligent, happy, together, intimidating, or fearless? Notice and then relax past these things. Purposefully allow the "real you" to come forth simply by standing there, maintaining the eye contact and resisting fear's impulses. Let go of pretenses and reveal those things which you fear will bring rejection.

This is the sharing of our private thoughts and ideas about ourselves as written in the body. State out loud your fears of being judged as you do this. Ask your partner beforehand to simply receive your communication with unconditional acceptance. Stay with it; eventually the fears will melt away. Notice your body language—you will probably find yourself wanting to cross your arms, keep a certain distance, laugh, talk, or avert your gaze. These are your defenses. Again, wait for them to relax as you uncross your arms, move in closer, and keep your gaze fixed in silence.

Once you have relaxed and are feeling more comfortable with being seen by the other, begin to see him (or her) for who *he* really is, looking for the shift in perception that reveals he is the same as you. He has the same dreams, hopes, disappointments, pains, and underneath it all, the same Love, the same quest for Joy. With this, you may notice that you naturally want good things for him. Look for this response. See all the years of history and struggle, his unmet dreams, his hopes and hurts, and look for the compassion that naturally comes forth in you for him. What do you want for him? What do you want for humanity?

When you are practicing this with someone who also wants to share his private thoughts, you can say to each other every thought, fear, and judgment that comes up in you about the other and have him do the same with you, back and forth. This can be used as a way of working out any misunderstandings, hurts, or blocks in communication. No matter what the difference of opinion, you will both recognize that the other is really coming from his quest for Truth, from his desire to have things work out well. In the end, everything is forgivable once understood. If we are "doing wrong," the other person can point out to us that, while our intention was to promote Joy, we may actually have been coming from a subtle fear and defending against it. The same is true, of course, for him. Bringing it all out, the fear is exposed and the need to impose our wishes upon reality is again released.

Another variation on the theme is to look into a mirror with one or more other people (or take a video of yourselves), so that you see who you are in relationship, how you project your ideas about yourself into the world "out there." Again, you will want to talk it all out, all your fears of not being accepted, approved of, and so on. Be prepared for some real surprises as you see how different your perception of yourself is in the mirror versus in your head. This can give a direct contact with the way fear distorts our perception as we realize we have been seeing ourselves through defense-colored glasses, trying to be someone we are not.

And finally, you can practice a type of "reparenting," where you dare to express your needs, like a child with its parent(s), and ask for the other(s) to fulfill your request. This is something we are almost universally trained, out of fear, to repress. And yet, the need goes on in subterranean realms. If we bring out this need, getting it filled where possible, it spends itself and no longer calls out for attention in unhealthy ways.

Look for the fear that kept you from asking for what you needed as a child and dare to ask for it now. If your fear was one of being rejected or abandoned, dare to ask for the caretaking, safety, and nurturing you have been seeking. Let yourself feel the vulnerability of a child, completely dependent on its parents. If your fear was of standing on your own, moving away from security, ask your "parents" to give you the support you have been needing to do so.

Of course, it will be necessary to set up the space in advance and let the others know what you are trying to accomplish, in order to get their agreement. They may feel too inhibited to support you in the way they would otherwise like to. Let them know that is okay with you and have alternatives set up. You will have to overcome your inhibitions as well, facing the fear of what the other person may think and how they may reject you if you dare to ask for such things. But in saying everything that you're afraid to say about this—about what they may think of you, who you really are, what you really want—you give the other person the chance to come to compassion and the spontaneous desire to give.

Just as important, if the other person agrees to be the child, is the act of being the "parent" so that you may experience the desire to give as well. If it helps, decide beforehand that you will each request three things from the other. That way, the fear of asking is lessened since you are *supposed* to find three things, and the worry that you will appear greedy or demanding is taken care of.

## Exercise 3: "Squeezing Out" Blocked Energy

Fear, as we have seen, has us jamming energy into a dead-end rut, in the attempt to force reality to look the way we want. When we restrict the free flow of energy in this way, it creates a blockage in thought *and* body; i.e., the energy that supplies our thoughts is jammed in a way that creates a physical jamming as well. Therefore, as we learn to release this blocked energy, we can expect that the thoughts it was fueling will be released simultaneously.

One of the primary places energy gets jammed when we are using the body to express our fears is in the diaphragm. The diaphragm plays a central role in the mechanics of breathing, and breathing plays a central role in the physical expression of fear and Joy. Further, the diaphragm is the muscle that pushes out the sound created by vibrating vocal cords, the audible expression of who we are. But most of all, the diaphragm is the primary seat for stored tension. To release the blocked energy of our fear, we must release the tension in the diaphragm.

Begin by visualizing the diaphragm as a deep reservoir of jammed-up energy which you want to push out, squeeze out, with all your might. Then, take a full breath in, and while not quite holding your breath but giving yourself the necessary resistance, press out, long and hard. Drain all the energy being held inside. Really squeeze the diaphragm, contract the stomach muscles, and push out the blocked energy. Let your face turn red, your body shake, and your deep Self pour forth. Repeat the process as many times as necessary.

It is important not to hold your breath completely while pressing out—this can increase blood pressure too much. You will be essentially holding your breath while squeezing out a little bit of air the whole way through. Also be careful about any physical injuries you have which this may exacerbate. The diaphragm is to be highly tensed in this exercise, but don't forget to pay attention to areas of injury which need to be protected.

You may want to make a long, loud sound as you squeeze the diaphragm. Your arms and even legs may want to squeeze or press against something as well. You are opening up the wellspring of tension when you open up the diaphragm, and the whole body may become involved. Follow its lead without hurting yourself. Let it do what it knows best how to do— relieve your tension, drain out the fear. Push past any resistance and push past the thought that says "that's enough."

You will be bringing up a great deal of emotion with this process, emotion which wants to be released and no longer squashed. You can encourage this by thinking about those issues which have been troubling you, or those issues which spontaneously arise as you open up the diaphragm in this way. Continue until your emotional expression feels complete. A good rule of thumb is to continue until you are thoroughly spent and your body collapses into relaxation, well beyond the point when you originally wanted to stop.

When finally your well is exhausted, simply sit and wait, without thinking, without moving, preferably with your eyes closed. After a few moments of resting, you will want to look for a new insight or a new way of perceiving some situation which has been troubling you. This is the shift in mind that accompanies that of the body.

Focusing on the diaphragm in this way is just the beginning of physical release; it will open up many possibilities for further cleansing. Some enhancements to this technique include the following: After initially squeezing the diaphragm, try pounding on or squeezing a pillow while making sound. If you are working with a specific issue, then let the sound come out with particular words or phrases (keep them short and to the point) that capture the essence of your release, such as "I will not let you stop me anymore!" or "I need you." Again, let your intuition, your body's wisdom, guide you, fully expressing whatever comes to mind.

This exercise can be done just as effectively when nothing is especially troubling you; it is a great idea to make a daily habit of cleansing your "system."

You may well feel the need to cry after such a release. This can be a most important part of the process and should always be encouraged. To help with this, you will want to get in a seated position and lean forward after you have finished squeezing the diaphragm, letting the upper body go limp and drape over the legs. Alternatively, you can get on your knees and elbows with your forehead or the top of your head touching the floor. Both of these positions free the diaphragm to contract and convulse in the release of crying.

You can, at the same time, begin a little bit of fast breathing to mobilize the energy, if needed. This will energize the blockages in the bodymind that have been jammed up, building the pressure until it seeks a release. There are many practices available today based on the use of rapid or altered breathing, from the ancient Hindu practice of pranayama to neo-Reichian breathing. Some of these have the participant breathing deeply and rapidly for several hours! Their effect is the same: To energize the emotions held in muscular memory, and move them through the blockages. These techniques should not, however, be performed without a trained facilitator. In this exercise, simply try perhaps ten to twenty fast breaths to supply a bit of extra energy to your process. This should be enough to evoke the desired reaction.

Finally, you can enhance the effect of squeezing out the energy blocked in the diaphragm by having someone press down hard, perhaps very hard (without causing pain) on your diaphragm, as you simultaneously press up against the hand with all your might, squeezing the diaphragm, making a loud and long noise to enhance the effect if possible. If you are in a place where you have to be concerned about others hearing you, simply bury your face in a pillow. This will damp the sound so that only you can hear it.

## Exercise 4: Whole-Body Approaches to Well-Being

Freeing up our self-expression in the voice, face, and our body's movements makes it possible to communicate who we truly are with a much wider repertoire. The limits on our self-expression are held in place by fear. When we learn to move in healthier and more natural ways, our fear is joyously released.

In the doorway of the body, we face our fears by physically doing the opposite of what fear would have us do. Therefore, in this exercise, we want to practice ways of expressing ourselves through the body that are outside the range of our usual personality style. For example, if we hold a face that is tightly controlled, showing no emotion, then we want to practice "loosening up." Someone who has learned to be "poker-faced" will want to practice opening their eyes more widely and using the eyebrows in a greater variety of ways. Someone who carries a "stiff upper lip" as a necessary protection will want to practice increasing the range of motion in their mouth. The rest of the body will naturally become involved as the extension of the new gestures written on our faces. This, of course, should be encouraged.

The voice is used as a center of control as well, modulating with great finesse the amount of emotion that comes through. For this, we want to vary the tonality and volume of our vocal expressions. Practice putting rich inflection in your voice, playing with higher- and lower-pitched sounds. Express different styles of personality in your voice, such as the innocence of a child, the competence of a master, or the enthusiasm of lovers. Be prepared for a significant confrontation with your fear as you do so—you will be surprised to discover how much our range of expression is limited to fixed patterns, and how difficult it can be to open up to other possibilities.

Think of the difference between the expressiveness of young children and a character like Mr. Spock, whose only demonstration of emotion is the lifting of a single eyebrow as he utters in a perfect monotone the word "fascinating." This is fine for a Vulcan but, when written on the face of a human, can only be the fear of expressing ourselves and letting others see who we really are. Let us throw caution to the wind as we let our true selves be known. To quote Whitman, let us "sound [our] barbaric yawp over the rooftops of the world"!

Think also of the character played by David Carradine in the old television show "Kung Fu." His every word, inflection, and movement were carefully and meaningfully chosen, a meditative prayer of intention in the tiniest gesture. This is the body language of a master! No fears were forcing him to express certain images of self and repress others. Fully in control of what he chose to convey, his communications were complete, exact, and deeply meaningful.

## Exercise 5: Psychodrama

If our experience of the physical world is but the projection of our thoughts into perception, then in relating to the physical world, we are truly relating only to the representations of people and situations in our minds. Psychodrama is the literal manifestation of this projection process, so that we may rewrite the script and act out a more joyous conclusion.

In psychodrama, we have the opportunity to play out the thoughts we are projecting onto the world in a conscious way. Originally masterminded by J. L. and Z. T. Morena, psychodrama involves acting out significant scenes from our lives, scenes which hold the critical moments of choice for fear or Joy. We then redesign these scenes according to the principles of healing. We literally stage the stories that have lived in our minds, using real people to enact the drama, making the mental experience physical.

This is the conscious playing out of the projection process we undertook in separating from Oneness, creating the world of perception in which we believe we live. The opportunity to project our thoughts *while being aware that we are doing so* holds great potential for healing, making it possible to redraw the script and discover our ability to create a new experience.

The power of this tool, however, can be had only if we create the scene in a way that evokes the feelings—fear in its many disguises—that seem to be out of our control. This, then, becomes the work, to focus on the moment or moments which evoke such feelings and face the fears that have been projected out in undesirable ways. In facing the fears, of course, we watch the illusion of their threat dissolve. And with this we find that we have been directing the show in our minds all along, and can now redirect it in a way that doesn't stop for imagined fears.

The how-to of psychodrama is simple: Find the scene you want to act out and cast your actors to play the significant roles. Tell them first what the story is about, then coach them very specifically in the words, mannerisms, and actions which will bring their characters to life for you.

You will play yourself in the psychodrama, not to repeat the same unhappy performance as before, but to watch yourself in the process of responding to fear in the ways your chief defense directed. Now, you are the director of your play and the play is your life! Find the new response that will set you free in this situation, facing the fear by doing precisely what it said not to do. You can explore all options, saying what you did not dare to say before, doing what you did not dare to do before. You can risk any response because the actual people and circumstances are not involved. You are simply working with the projections of your own mind.

A process called sculpting can be very helpful here. Sculpting involves creating symbolic placements, postures, gestures, key phrases, and interactions that capture the critical emotions of the scene. For example, if someone has betrayed you in the scene you are re-creating, you may direct the actor playing the part to literally turn his or her back on you at the appropriate time, so that you may relive your feelings and respond in a new way. Alternatively, you might practice turning your back on someone you have been too dependent on, in the interest of facing your fear, and experience what it is like to leave that person behind. If you feel stopped in life from reaching your goal, try directing the others to create a blockade with their bodies, keeping you from reaching the other side where your goal is waiting. Your job could be to find a way through the blockade, physically putting yourself through the experience of your fear. Of course, you will want to direct the actors to make it safe enough for you to be able to succeed in your task.

As in a theatrical production, you can set up a "tableau," a picture which captures the feeling of the scene without words, people placed in the symbolic positions which represent their relationship to each other and to you. For example, a domineering father and a passive mother may be positioned as follows: The father stands in an imposing way, towering over the others while the mother cowers, kneeling at his feet, half turned away from you. Or if your parents perhaps caught you up in a triangle, jockeying for your attention to satisfy their own needs, you may create the scene where they are each on one side of you, pulling at you in opposite directions.

And of course, words can be used to externalize the feelings you have in this scene. Find the right key phrases, phrases which the characters in the story actually said or perhaps phrases which catch the essence of the interaction. If a phrase is powerful enough, it can be repeated several times, either by you or the other people, to evoke the necessary feelings and abreactions. Universal phrases such as "Leave me alone," "I'm angry at you," "I need you," or "I love you," to name just a few, are usually behind such scenes. These are actually expressions of the core fear, and to know your core fear and dare to say it at the right moment can be exceptionally powerful.

As you go through the psychodrama, you will feel emotions that you may need to express physically. As in Exercise 3, have a pillow nearby to pound or squeeze out your feelings and practice opening up your voice and daring to move in ways your fear said not to before. Sculpt the scene in a way that physically represents your new understanding of yourself and the others involved. You might, for example, now want to rise up from cowering underneath the authority figure and express your fearlessness by standing face-to-face or side-by-side with him.

Sculpting can also be very fulfilling as a conclusion to the psychodrama, setting things up the way you always wanted them to be. You can create the experience of your family standing close together with you in the middle, go head to head with your boss as you practice asserting yourself, or leave your old world behind as you move out of that circle and walk forward into a new life.

Psychodrama is a rich and subtle tool. A trained facilitator can, perhaps, help you take this work much farther than you can do on your own. Nevertheless, its healing potential is still and always in its ability to help you face your fear. This is something anyone can do. All that is necessary is that you evoke the fear and do the opposite of what it says to do, the opposite of what the chief defense directs. If you cannot find enough other people to play out the scene with you, then have one other person play various parts, or the most significant part. You can also do this by yourself, talking it out in the mirror or writing it out in a journal. The point is to externalize, in concrete, physical form, the projections of your mind, and confront the fears that have been driving you.

# CHAPTER 6

# THE DOORWAY OF THE SPIRIT

"Come to the cliff," he said. "We are afraid," they said.
"Come to the cliff," he said. They came. He pushed
them. And they flew.

—Stuart Wilde

Viktor Frankl was a Viennese psychiatrist who lived through the horrors of the Nazi concentration camps. In his time there, he discovered that no matter what the circumstances we find ourselves in, no matter how horrific, we can make a choice for Joy. When his clothing, his dignity, his identity, and a precious manuscript, his life's work, were taken from him, he felt that he had nothing left to live for. Every day in the camp he witnessed people throwing themselves against the electrified fence, and with the loss of his manuscript, he realized that he, too, was confronted with the choice of whether to live or to die.

When finally he contracted typhoid, he saw how easy it would be simply to stop eating, not try to get well, and give up his will to live. But in that moment, he made a decision to begin rewriting his manuscript. He would write it on sheets of toilet paper, hiding it under the floorboards when the guards walked by. He had found his purpose again; he began to get well.

That manuscript became a most penetrating book, *Man's Search for Meaning*. It spawned an entire school of psychotherapy called "logotherapy," an existential philosophy built on the idea that to find one's meaning, a higher life Purpose, is to find a great cure for our suffering.

He recalls, for example, certain prisoners in the camps who, instead of becoming preoccupied with their own suffering, found the will to live by comforting others, perhaps offering their last piece of bread to those with a greater need, or giving encouragement to those who had fallen into despair. From this, he learned the great truth "that everything can be taken from a man but one thing: the last of the human freedoms— to choose one's attitude in any given set of circumstances, to choose one's own way." It is this choice, he says, which determines whether we become "the plaything of circumstance" or whether *we* decide "what shall become of [us]— mentally or spiritually. . . . [With this, we] may retain [our] human dignity even in a concentration camp."

Later, Frankl tells the story of a young woman he attended as she approached her death. Coming to peace with her experience in the camp she said, " 'I am grateful that fate has hit me so hard. . . . In my former life I was spoiled and did not take spiritual accomplishments seriously.' Pointing through the window of the hut, she said, 'This tree here is the only friend I have in my loneliness.' Through that window she could see just one branch of a chestnut tree, and on the branch were two blossoms. 'I often talk to this tree,' she said to me. I was startled and didn't quite know how to take her words. Was she delirious? Did she have occasional hallucinations? Anxiously I asked her if the tree replied. 'Yes.' What did it say to her? She answered, 'It said to me, "I am here—I am here— I am life, eternal life".' "

What is it that impels us to face our fear? We could do it

through the sheer joy of finding our Good. More often, we resist this, defending against it with our minds and with our bodies, until the pain becomes too great and we can no longer keep our illusions going.

It is said that eighty percent or more of our suffering comes from such resistance, as we attempt to exercise control, protecting against pain and loss, and holding on to the possibility of fulfilling our separate identities. In fact, the entire world of our suffering emerges from the idea that there is something needing to be controlled at all. We want to control other people, ourselves, and reality. We want to force the "world out there" to conform to our idea of what would make us safe and happy. When the world does not comply, we suffer.

When finally we have had enough, we will naturally come to the breaking point and let go. Recognizing that fear's strategy for keeping us safe has never truly worked, we see through the illusion that "just one more try" will do the trick. We forfeit our investment in the "joy" of separation, divesting ourselves of a separate identity at odds with the rest. The true Self then emerges, unobstructed by the contracted focus of self-interest, to join with the All which is One.

This is the doorway of the spirit, where we identify with that in us which is bigger than fear, transcending fear's concerns. We place our attention instead on an ultimate sense of Meaning and Purpose in which the many lessons of human experience are understood in their larger context. The old world of our misunderstanding dries up as we no longer energize it with our fear, and everywhere we turn we see the evidences of Joy.

## Peter

A 29-year-old man named Peter came to see me because of his interest in spiritual growth. He had heard a lecture I gave and wanted guidance. Originally, he had his path in life all "figured out"; he just couldn't understand why it wasn't working.

After building a therapeutic trust in which he knew I was committed to his growth, he allowed me to confront his strategy. He had been working for several years, with a fierce intensity, to transcend the limits of his humanness, and almost force a spiritual awakening. He had a particular love for the ways of St. Francis and wanted to "go out on the streets" to "bring spirituality to people," to "make them understand" the importance of these matters. One day, while in an especially fiery state, he declared he wanted to "take the plunge," giving up all security to pursue his spiritual work, not delaying any longer for the "mundaneness of the world."

Finding my opportunity, I offered him a line from *A Course in Miracles:* "Only infinite patience produces immediate effects." He was truly confronted. His whole idea of how to succeed spiritually was being exposed as the problem, not the solution. His impatience to reach spiritual heights was the very thing keeping him stuck on the ground.

In the peak of his discomfort, I quietly said, "Let go, Peter." With this he looked at me in near-panic, the "death throes" of his ego. Closing his eyes, he moved into an expanded state. Intensity was written all over his face until finally he cried out, "There is no more 'me'; there is no more 'Peter.' " His whole body was taut and poised at attention, with the earnestness of one who was peering into higher realms.

Finally he relaxed, fully spent. After a few minutes he opened his eyes and told me what had happened. "I felt like I went through the tunnel they talk about when you die, and came out the other side into a white light. And in the light was this incredible peace. I realized then that I don't have to work so hard, I don't have to fight anymore. I don't have to work hard to earn my spirituality, I already have it and it can't be taken away."

Since that time, he has allowed a flow and an ease into his

life with a natural spirituality that he describes as "something bigger than me; it 'does' me, I don't have to 'do' it."

Peter, as much as his words and behaviors looked spiritual, had been using his spirituality as a defense. In attempting to change the world through *his* ideas of what should be, he was, in fact, seeking to control, to escape his fear of dealing with the challenges of everyday life. As we let go of fear and defensiveness, we no longer need to control or escape anything, but are free to embrace the whole of life in all its complexity. This is true spirituality, the natural result of letting go of fear.

Until his transformation, Peter would continue to exercise his defense of control, even when his path was not working. He was insisting that his ideas were appropriate and true, that they would "make things work better." And he was ready to take drastic measures if necessary to prove his point.

This insistence on control, on seeing what we want to see, on trying to make reality what we want it to be, is the source of our suffering. In our fear, we would hold fast to the idea that only *our* dream of happiness can satisfy us. The rest of reality, everything that doesn't agree with this, must be defended against at all costs. We devote ourselves to making enough money, having the right "things," wearing the right attributes, and on and on and on, trying to fulfill a predetermined ideal of what would give us Joy. The means become the end, our efforts taking on full-time proportions, never allowing us to rest and enjoy the results. And reality goes on uninterrupted all the while, presenting the true secret to fulfillment by virtue of its original Joy, waiting for us to take it up on its terms.

Again, this insistence on forcing things to fit our ideals is the whole reason for our suffering. For every time reality fails to agree with what we insist it should be, our whole structure for living, our understanding of how things work, our very identity threatens to collapse. Instead of a quiet acceptance of what is, we busily set about trying to control with our defenses all the more strongly. This is why surrender is touted as the prerequisite to Enlightenment; we must surrender our attempts to control reality and take our place in the natural flow of things.

This Zen parable illustrates the point: A man walking across a field encounters a tiger. Terrified, he flees, the tiger chasing after him. He soon comes to a cliff and swings himself over the side, hanging on to a branch just out of the tiger's reach. Two mice, one white and one black, begin gnawing at the branch. Down below, another tiger waits hungrily. Suddenly, the man sees a big, luscious strawberry just to his left. Hanging from the branch with his right hand, he reaches out and plucks the strawberry. How sweet it tasted!

This is being in the moment, surrendering our personal designs upon reality and following the flow of reality-as-it-is. It is the key to Freedom because, with no need to control or change anything about reality-as-it-is, there is nothing that would imprison us, nothing we must fight against, nothing we would perceive as threatening to our Joy.

Let us put this in terms of our present work. When we decided to separate from Oneness, we sought an experience where we could have "more." We wanted it "all for ourselves." Our solution for dreaming this experience would be to see ourselves as "individuals" with the right to design a reality different from Oneness, a reality where only what we chose to see would be real. In this way, we could deny the Oneness and see the reality of our making.

All meanings, then, would be based on what we wanted to see; everything would be given its value according to how well it promoted our goal. The core fear would become that of losing our individuality, our "right" to be separate and accomplish our own wishes. Anything "outside" of us would be interpreted as a threat, for knowing that it was one with us, we would build our defenses against it in order to maintain our separate identity. And we would suffer whenever we could not be certain of success, feeling deprived of what we wanted for ourselves. The idea of joining with the whole would threaten our "instinct" for self-preservation, as we imagined the dissolution of who we thought we were into a void of Oneness.

This is the process we have been engaged in ever since. This is the human condition. Unless we are experiencing ourselves at one with the whole of reality, we are in fear, busily thinking up ways to control. We then build the defenses that would try to change reality, keeping out what we do not like, forcing our wishes upon the rest. We literally refuse to see what we do not want to see, and insist upon seeing what we prefer instead.

Undoing this is a matter of facing the fear, surrendering the control, that launched the process to begin with. In the doorway of the mind, we accomplished this by penetrating the thoughts we had in response to the fear. In the doorway of the body, we worked through the projections of these thoughts onto the body and the world. Here, in the doorway of the spirit, we will rise above the thoughts, letting go the need to engage the entire process in the first place, identifying with the spirit, or "pure consciousness," that lives behind the thoughts and gives them their life.

This is the high road to Joy, dissolving the illusion of fear at its very source. It requires nothing less than the complete surrender of our personal wishes when they are at odds with the greater Good. But our practice has brought us to the point where we are realizing that the only thing we truly surrender is an illusion of control and the pain that came with it. Such a surrender brings the reward we were trying to create with our control all along, as pain and disappointment fall away and Joy is restored, whole, complete, and unbroken.

## The Mastery of Thoughts

The meditative traditions from all faiths and spiritualities teach about the mastery of thoughts. By "mastery" we mean detaching from thoughts, choosing them consciously or sitting without thoughts altogether. In essence, we mean not being run by our thoughts, where they seem to tell us what to do, how to feel, and what to think next. We are, the Buddhists say, like "a drunken monkey stung by a bee," frenetically chasing impulses, whims, and fantasies. We want to take back our mind so that it may serve our higher Purpose.

We can classify two main approaches to the mastery of thought: penetration and transcendence. In penetration, we enter into the thought and, instead of getting caught up in it, see through its illusion of "realness," piercing its veil of independent existence to understand it as something we have created. In transcendence, we detach from our thoughts, witnessing them from on high, and do not comply with their demand to follow them.

Similarly, we may identify two types of meditation, two ways of moving toward these goals. In one, the meditator practices what is sometimes called "one-pointed attention," where thoughts are focused upon a single object. The mind develops a concentrative power to choose where it places its attention. Following the breath, saying the rosary, liturgical chanting, Sufi dikr, and repeating the mantra are all means toward this same end.

In the second, the meditator is to empty the mind of thoughts, identifying with the thinker and not the thoughts, until even the thought of the thinker disappears.

Whatever the strategy, we must get "behind" our thoughts, surrendering our attempts to control through thinking. We enter into the realm of the spirit where we are no longer bound by the world our thinking has generated. Again in Buddhism, we are told there are 70,000 thoughts per second. The mind, with its cascade of thoughts, is described as a waterfall. Try meditating, if you are not already practiced, on following the breath and only the breath. With a little honesty, you will notice that you are not yet able to do so for more than a second or two before the thoughts start pouring in, seemingly out of control. And this we do every moment of our lives.

We do not have to be bound to our thoughts. As the twelve-step programs are fond of saying, we can refuse to let anybody or anything "rent space in our heads." Our thoughts are the noise which would distract us from the stillness and peace of Joy. This noise is generated by fear. And as with any fear, it can be faced and released. In a meditation, a patient with whom I was working witnessed her thoughts rising, living out their lives and dying away in slow motion. Every one of them had to do with a mental checklist of fear: Was the stove turned off? Would she get to her next appointment on time? What if she were to make a deeper commitment to her spiritual life and leave her present responsibilities? Watching these thoughts float by without attachment, they lost their hold and she moved into the Peace of the present moment, where none of these fears was truly happening.

But, we ask, wouldn't everything be chaos if we did not try to think our way into order and meaning? We have already looked at the arbitrary nature of the meanings we impose on reality. This is the voice of fear, again, attempting to control in order to create its preferred view. Without our self-imposed thoughts, nothing would obstruct our view of reality-as-it-is. Giving up the control we falsely assume with our thinking does not lead to chaos. We are simply giving up something that never was truly ours, and letting ourselves relax into the acceptance that brings peace. We cannot push the river, as the Native Americans say, but we can allow it to take us smoothly where it will. And this is always a joyous destination.

## Surrender and the Controlling Ego

There is a story in the opening of Richard Bach's *Illusions* which tells of a colony of certain shrimp-like creatures. These creatures spend their entire socialization reinforcing the idea that they must cling desperately to the side of a rock wall, lest they be swept away by the "current." Finally, one of them dares to challenge this assumption and, amid the horror and warnings of the others, lets go of the rock wall. At first thrashed wildly to and fro by the untamed current, he then settles into its flow and, as if flying, is carried effortlessly through incredible vistas and new territories, participating in the variety of what life has to offer. (Of course, the shrimp-like creatures downstream who see him flying by without clinging determine that he must, in fact, be a Messiah!)

The Buddhist idea of letting go of attachments is the same as letting go of fears; we attach to that which, in our fear, we believe we must control. Nowhere is this more evident than in the attachment to our identity, our idea of who we are. But who we think we are is an invention, a made-up self constructed for the purpose of seeing ourselves as powerful over the forces of reality, able to control and get what we want. The devices we use toward this end are themselves false assumptions—repression, denial, projection—attempts to change what is. The key to Enlightenment is found in letting go of all attachment to false ideas about who we are and what reality is. When we do so, we will see things revealed in their original nature, without imposed projection, and discover the true experience of Joy.

The twelve-step programs are similar in ideology. In fact, the words "addiction" and "attachment" are interchangeable. The first of the twelve steps requires that a person "admits she is powerless" over the source of her addiction. This is the recognition that our thoughts are futile; the addict uses such thoughts to convince herself that she is in control and she knows the best way to manage life. Notice the attempt, again, to make reality the way we wish it to be, refusing to acknowledge reality-as-it-is.

We can, thankfully, save ourselves from this fate by getting wise to the process and taking this same step. Recognizing that, operating from fear's premise, we have never truly reached our goal, we see through the illusion of it and admit our powerlessness. And with this, we can surrender our attraction to fear, to separation, with quiet confidence and grace.

When we say that something about reality is not acceptable, when we impose our wishes and reject, repress, or deny the way things are, we create the separation all over again. For when we reject something, we defend against our idea of it, insulate ourselves from it, and build a protective wall to keep it out. But in building this wall we define our idea about what has been rejected as a "real" entity; it is now defined as that which is on the other side of the wall and that which must stay there. And in being defined this way, it takes on meaning and life. In our responding to it, we make the definition real, for there must be something real causing our response. The more we try to push it away, the more real it becomes. It gathers the strength we give it, increasing in its vitality to push back. In reality, all we need do is surrender our resistance and the whole idea will shrivel up and wither away into the nothingness it always was.

## Giving Up the Fight Against Reality

This is why all defenses backfire. They are designed to try to make us "safe" from what we have wrongly imagined would take away our happiness. They are designed to make only what we think we want real; all the rest must be defended against. And this backfires because we must then be on guard forevermore, never able to relax and enjoy the freedom from threat our defenses are supposed to bring. Instead we make the threat all the more real, something to be on guard about, something to imagine is about to strike so we can be ready for it.

In the doorway of the spirit, the way to undo this, the facing of the fear, is to no longer fight against reality. Instead of trying to make it "go away," thereby perpetuating the belief that it is "bad," "wrong," and must be "fixed," we move toward it, doing the opposite of what our fear says to do. We do not fight against it but befriend it, accepting it as it is. And in accepting it, we accept ourselves, knowing our true spiritual stature as that which can fearlessly accept all things.

For we recognize that who we already are, spiritually, is so much bigger than our fear that there never was anything to fight against. Enlightenment is simply the seeing of things as they truly are, as part of reality, without the intervention of fear's thoughts. And without these thoughts, we see there is nothing to fix or change or even heal. All that is needed is the awareness that this is so.

We must recognize this in all parts of reality. As a spiritual teacher once said, we will not go "Home" until every last corner of fear is swept clean. We must recognize this with all parts of ourselves we have considered unacceptable. This is the secret to health—sickness results when we cut off a part of ourselves, defending against some aspect of who we are. Further, we must do this with all parts of other people, for indeed they are parts of ourselves as well. And we must do this with all parts of the world, to see that everything participates in a Oneness and nothing is alien to us. We no longer, then, are concerned that something, some part of "us," can be taken away. In this lies the end of fear.

So our work is to find and face fear, to catch and let go fear's thoughts and the defenses we build up around them. We want to accept things-as-they-are instead of reaching for a happiness defined by personal wishes. This is the new goal of life, to discover that defenselessness *does* bring safety. The only requirement is the willingness to face our fears.

We want to be willing to face our fears wherever we find them. We want to be willing to sit in the "anxiety" of letting go of control, giving up our efforts for safety and comfort when they come at the expense of Truth. We want to be willing to sit in this anxiety (energy? power? excitement?) forever, if need be, and find the "immediate results" that come with infinite patience. Only in this can we have the real control that is perfect freedom, and come to know the Joy of reality-as-it-is.

This is the final surrender. We go about with secret dreams for what we want our lives to look like, who we want to be, how we want to be glorified, and a tremendous force of will to "get" things to be this way. Only when we surrender these plans can we find real Joy. And to surrender is really a matter of admitting to our powerlessness over such things, admitting that we do not, in truth, have such power.

*A Course in Miracles* describes us, in our attempt to control, as a little ripple thinking it is the ocean or a tiny sunbeam thinking it is the sun. We want to practice remembering that our efforts to control reality have never gotten us lasting Joy. In the end, whatever happiness we may have won through these maneuvers gives way to pain and disappointment.

Let us, then, choose the release and relief, the peace and flow waiting for us when we give up the fight against the universe. If all we really care about is Joy, we must recognize that in our efforts to obtain it we have been inserting ourselves it its way. We want to practice a graceful flow with the river, allowing ourselves to be taken by our good, instead of trying to push and control to make it flow the way we want. For only when we give up the attempt to have things turn out as *we* decide they should be can we harness the energy of Joy, directing it so that all things may turn out as they should.

There is indeed a tremendous power that comes with surrender. Without investment in particular outcomes, nothing can hold or own us. This is the true meaning of Freedom. And with it comes the energy, uninhibited by fear, to express Joy without limit. Our way is unobstructed and we now can drink up the fullness of Life, the mystery of Creation, so infinitely wondrous that, once tasted in even the slightest way, it dissolves all fear into nothingness.

## The Transcendent Spirit

There is a story about a "bound man." This man, having been sentenced for a crime he did not commit, was chained to a prison wall in punishment. He thrashed and strained against his shackles until his wrists and ankles bled, outraged at being so confined. After some time, his strength left him, and he fell into a deep despair.

After many years it was discovered that he had been wrongly accused. Immediately, the people went forth to set him free. As the prison chains were unlocked, all watched in expectation, waiting for him to celebrate his release. But instead, he stayed where he was, quietly, without moving. For he had long ago found his freedom within.

All the great teachers have shown us this truth. The Buddha, when very close to his Enlightenment, was seduced by fear in all its "glory." Wild fantasies flashed across his mind: 10,000 armies shooting flaming arrows, huge lightning bolts, thunder-filled skies, and tidal waves—the most terrifying images of destruction all tempted him to self-protection and the belief in fear. But having surrendered such beliefs, he was looking past such illusions. In all calmness, he touched the earth, as if to declare his rootedness in what is real. The flaming arrows turned to lotus petals, falling gently at his feet.

St. Francis, too, would physically wrestle with "devils," projections of his fear, and seek out opportunities to impoverish himself. Poverty, for him, became something that brought him closer to God. "Holy Poverty!" It was his Beloved. Personified as a beautiful woman in rags, he took it to mean his freedom from the egoistic attention to material security. Similarly, he looked forward to the chance to be publicly humiliated. He relished it. The more he did so, the more he would strip away his concern for approval, and the more his heart was free for God. An unusual path to surrender, but effective!

And Jesus, of course, consciously took on the extreme example of surrender, being mocked, scourged, and crucified, to demonstrate that even the greatest assault to a self-made identity cannot force compliance with fear. In the midst of such complete and utter "ruin," his attention was on the suffering of his "persecutors" and their need for comfort. In a supreme act of "self"lessness, he says "Father, forgive them for they know not what they do."

When our passion for and commitment to Joy are strong enough, we can bypass the fear in our mind and its projections onto the body, going straight for the transcendent fulfillment of the spirit. The doorway of the spirit is opened when we are so filled with a high Purpose, with Joy, that we are willing to surrender all other purposes, knowing that they, in fact, rob us of our Joy, no matter how much they seem to promise.

This "surrender of all other purposes" characterizes the final stage of our transformation. Giving up our defenses, admitting that we cannot control reality, we relinquish our attempt to force it to comply with our wishes and say, "Let it be as You [Joy], not I, would have it." With this, we are free and available to see the perfection of all things just as they are, without the overlay of fear. We give up the fight that was no fight, surrender that which never existed. For, truly, in our surrender, we discover that the only thing that was keeping us from the Joy we seek was our refusal to accept it. It is all around, waiting but for our acknowledgment.

# EXERCISES

In the doorway of the spirit, we get inspired past our fear. With the invigorating effect of high Purpose, the attraction of the spirit, it is easy to withdraw our attention from fear and move into the eternal perspective of Joy. The fears of our lives shift into their right perspective, so small as to not be able to cause us concern, incapable of deceiving us any longer with the thought that they offer more than the Joy of the spirit.

We know ourselves in our true stature, infinitely bigger than fear, incapable of being threatened with the loss of anything that is really important. For we have what nothing of the world can give or take away: the awareness of who we truly are, connected with the whole, with everyone and everything else, secure in the experience of Oneness.

With this kind of fulfillment, we happily "give up our rights" to be a separated individual, taking for ourselves without regard for the whole, fending off the attack of others who would steal what we have taken. We happily give up our "righteous indignation" at not being honored as such an individual with rights. We eagerly surrender all concern with "self"-preservation, the endless struggle to preserve our separate identity. And we release the enormous and exhausting effort involved in maintaining this illusion, understanding that it was robbing us of the very Joy it promised to give.

With the infilling of spiritual Joy, we transcend our fears. The illusion of protection afforded by defenses dissolves. We rise "above the battleground," not detached from the world, but free from the fears of it that would have us living in defensive and unhappy ways. In fact, we are free to fully engage the world for the first time, acting from a Joy that is unrestrained by fear. Automatically and without effort, we heal others into this state as well, offering the Freedom we have found. We accept and therefore join with everything as it is, having no fearful concerns, giving up the need to protect and defend a separate sense of self.

This transcendence of fear is not different from finding and facing fear. Indeed, we must take care to discern the difference between true transcendence and the repression or denial of fear. In order for our transcendence to be real, we must be fully aware of our fear, seeing it and feeling it, stripping it of its false cloaking to expose its nakedness. Only then can we compare it to the power of the spirit and have it lose its meaning and threat, fading into nothingness in the comparison. This may happen in an instant, appearing to be a spontaneous enlightenment, but it still requires the facing of fear in the moment of awakening. If, therefore, it takes time and practice, so be it. We know the way and our success is ultimately assured.

## Giving Up Our Rights

In these exercises we practice what it means to "give up our rights," becoming so filled with Joy that the need to assert our rights disappears. Again, if we are to return to Oneness, we must give up our idea of being a separate individual. And only if we are a separate individual can we pretend to have rights that must be defended.

In truth, we don't really have these rights to give up; we don't have the "right" to be separate. This is not a moral judgment, a pronouncement of guilt for our presumption, but rather a statement of fact. It is said that we should not judge, not because it is a right to be taken away from us but simply because we are not really capable of judging accurately. In the calm recognition of truth, we realize that we don't possess these rights, they are not something we can own.

To understand why, we remember that we originally bought into fear as a way of trying to make reality different from what it is. We came out of the Oneness, thinking we could find something "more." We would "sacrifice" our perfect Joy for the sake of "self-glorification." We then projected the idea that our "right" to separate this way needed to be protected. We imagined a fearful entity—God, other people, an attacking world—that would try to take away this right, forcing us to return to Oneness. And so we became afraid.

But this was our deceit. *We* made up the idea that there was something to be afraid of, something "out there" that would take away what was never really ours because it never existed in the first place. Our fear, therefore, is an attempt to control that we may get what we want—the right to believe we are separate and can make reality different from what it is.

When we choose fear, we are attempting to defend against the thing we fear. Fear is a way of saying, "I'm afraid of reality the way it is; it should not be that way." When we are afraid of others, we are in effect telling them, "You are wrong for making me afraid, and I will make you feel guilty enough about it that you will change." In truth, we don't have the right to say anything should be other than the way it is. It simply is what it is, and no question of "should" or "should not" is relevant.

The same is true for all other names of fear. Anger, or hate, is also the attempt to control and force the reality we wish. Here is the seed problem of all our relationships; we seek out another person (or situation, thing, idea) which we believe will fulfill our fantasy of getting reality to be as we want it to be. In the honeymoon phase of our relationships, we feel the thrill of romantic love, for we believe we have finally achieved our goal. But the moment the other person fails to live up to our expectations, our requirements, really, they are outcast. They become the source of our unhappiness, and "eternal love" turns to hate. Hate, then, is the attempt to make the other feel guilty for causing our pain. This serves the dual purpose of trying to make her conform to our wishes once again, while further distracting us from the realization that we created the whole game.

Similarly, we must give up our right to attack, for our attack presumes that we have the right to impose our wishes and change what we are attacking. We might say that spirituality is the practice of giving up our attack on reality—the right to exercise anger, control, judgment—again, not because we "should" do this but because we recognize the truth of it. We recognize that our attack against reality is not in accord with the way of things and, in fact, has been causing our pain.

But even our spirituality can be used in the service of fear.

For in reaching for higher truths, in giving up our attack upon reality, we may be secretly avoiding the need to deal with things as they are. This can either come from the denial mentioned earlier, sometimes called a "spiritual bypass," or from using our spirituality to gain "power" over reality and force it to do our will. It is only when we give up both of these defenses that our spirituality can truly work and our Joy be sustained. This is why Meister Eckhard has said, "Man's last and highest parting is when, for God's sake, he takes leave of God."

This is also why we are reminded to practice not already knowing what a thing means. In believing that we already know what a thing means, we are trying to force it to be the way we say it should be. Moment-to-moment we try to dominate reality, assuming an authority we do not have, insisting that it conform to our wishes.

At the highest level, we must surrender all self-serving aims, releasing the illusion that we are separate from what we want. With this comes the joyous discovery that it was never taken away from us in the first place, for in the Oneness, we are literally joined with it all.

Facing fears is the antidote to such insanity and the prerequisite for spiritual transformation. It is the way we stop trying to change reality. For it is we who created the fears in the first place in the desire to experience something "more" than Oneness. Fear became our excuse to repress the Joy of things as they already were and therefore try to change reality. We erected our defenses, guard dogs at the gate of our fear, to hold back the desire to return to our original state. And it is with these defenses that we would force our will upon reality. But with Faith and Trust, loving assistants to surrender, we may give up such defenses, keeping our sights firmly set on Joy.

Only when we surrender the "right" to have these defenses and remember they have never truly fulfilled their promises; only when we think of the release and relief waiting for us when we give up our fight against the universe; only when we realize that all we want is Joy and that in our efforts to obtain it we have been inserting ourselves in the way; only when we gracefully flow with the river and allow ourselves to be taken by our Good, by the Universal Movement of Things, instead of trying to push and control to make things turn out the way we want—only then can we find true Joy, Freedom, Peace, and the return to Oneness at last.

In the exercises which follow, it is especially important to be aware of the possible fear that would have us do these exercises out of a need to "be good." *The only reason to give up our rights is because we recognize that doing so will bring Joy.* Do not use these exercises as another excuse for self-denial, self-deprivation, or the fear-based idea that suffering and sacrifice earn us "points" with God. In such cases, it is better, and just as viable, to reach for Joy through the doorways of the body and/or mind first. But if you are ready to take the more direct route, then these very powerful exercises can produce remarkable results. The key to success, again, is to keep your sights set firmly on Joy.

## Preparatory Exercise: Tools for Joy

The repertoire of tools for Joy from around the world and throughout time is a treasure chest of inspiration. The Sufi chants the names of God, the Jew davens at the Western Wall, the shaman whips him- or herself into an ecstatic state. There are snake-biting rituals, firewalking ceremonies, tarantellas, trance dances, and bacchanalia, all designed to help us tap into the space wherein Joy's higher perspective is remembered.

In this exercise, you will develop your own kit of tools for Joy. These are not to be considered transformative in their own right—unless we are also facing our fears, the Joy these tools can bring is at best temporary. Rather, they can help you remember your goal and reinvigorate your perspective when your commitment to Joy needs a boost. And they will be useful assists in the exercises which follow, keeping you in contact with your reason for engaging these practices.

Find several things you can do to call forth the taste of Joy. Listen to great music. Read some beautiful poetry. Get your juices flowing with some intensive physical exercise. Accomplish some task that cleans out the junk in your life. Dance, drum, sing, climb, swim! Create some inspiring artistic expression, witness a sunrise or a sunset, make love, or get out into Nature. Find specific actions you can take that enliven your spirit and clear away the thoughts and feelings of joylessness in a forcible way. Anything that brings you in touch with the quickening effect of a higher perspective is helpful.

One such practice involves simply pumping yourself up with the words, intonations, and energy of Joy, pouring on the juice and exclaiming your devotion to Joy with all the zeal and intensity you can muster. Get creative and invent your own ways of "turning on," so that the Joy you are reaching for is clearly in view as you go through the rest of these exercises. Call upon these tools on an "as needed" basis, making them an automatic habit so they are readily available whenever you need support along the way.

## Exercise 1: Giving Up Our Rights

The practice for this exercise involves building the association that says giving up our rights means getting closer to Joy. As we find and face the fear of giving up what we thought would make us happy, we give up the need to protect such happiness. We give up the need to defend what is "rightly" ours, requiring us to separate from imagined threats, isolating and cutting ourselves off from the connection we so desperately want.

In this way, self-defense, the protection of our rights, leaves us feeling bereft of what we truly need. It leaves us feeling lost to our wholeness, deprived of our Joy. This emptiness is filled in direct proportion to our defenselessness; that is, we fill up these holes exactly as much as we give up our rights. Give them up a little, perhaps letting go of a grievance against someone who ruffled your feathers, and you will feel a measure of relief and lightness. Give them up a lot, bypassing your insecurities and taking action on your highest ideals, and the spiritual excitement you feel will match the size of the fear you have faced. The more we give up our old ideas of how to find Joy, the more we clear the way to the real thing.

On a new page in your Workbook, practice inventing reasons, building the association, for why you want to give up your rights. As always we must first find the fear behind the "right" we want to transform. Begin, therefore, by listing on the left side of the page, *"Rights to Be Given Up."* Include those things you find yourself striving for, demanding, controlling, and insisting upon throughout your day and throughout your lifetime. On the right side of the page, write down your *"Reasons for Giving Them Up."* Find a higher spiritual purpose for being willing to let them go, have them fail, be taken away from you. In general, your reasons will be based on the recognition that insisting upon these rights has, in fact, caused you pain or tension or in some way deprived you of Joy, and that giving up these rights will release you from these problems. As you become ready, take action on these reasons, doing the opposite of what you thought you had the right to do, facing the fear of what you think will happen if you do not claim this right.

In looking for the rights you have been holding on to, think also about the right you thought you had to be angry, guilty, jealous, or even afraid. All of these, too, come from the sense of being a separate self. Whenever we feel like a victim of circumstances, we are trying to exercise the right to change these circumstances with the idea that we should not be made victim. As we have seen, we have created the idea of victim, so it can only be further manipulation to say that circumstances should not have done this to us.

This, I believe, is the true meaning of "If someone strikes you on the cheek, offer him the other one as well." It is not a call to self-denial which actually fosters the belief that the other did something wrong to us. Rather it is a recognition that letting go the need to "get back," even offering kindness in response to injury, demonstrates to us that we are free from the age-old cycle of attack and defense.

Feel the indignation that comes with the thought of offering the other cheek. Notice the rational arguments you come up with against it. These are the voices of fear, and they do in fact keep us prisoner. We can be glad, then, for the opportunity to see our fear in action and to get a feel for what it would be like to let it go. True, we do not want to take this approach if we cannot genuinely transform the feeling of having been slighted, diminished, or otherwise wronged. Nor are we to offer the other cheek if doing so objectively obstructs a higher purpose. But when someone injures our self-concept and presumes to take away our rights, we want to build the association that tells us this is a real gift.

St. Francis took this practice to an extreme. In his zeal for releasing pride, he would actively seek out opportunities to humiliate himself in public, eagerly looking for the chance to strip away his feeling of wanting to be liked, approved of, thought well of by others. He recognized such motivation as the trap that it was, and built a strong association between this kind of "humility" and the spiritual riches it would bring. In the same way, the chance to give away all his possessions, to fall in love with "Lady Poverty," to ask to be wounded like Christ in the crucifixion—all this freed him from the need to hold on to those things, both physical and conceptual, that would define him as a separate or "special" self.

For this exercise we use any means we can to become so filled with the promise of Joy that whatever we were holding on to out of fear no longer interests us. We need not go to such lengths as Francis to begin to find our Good. Any movement toward defenselessness is richly rewarded. Still, this path can seem steep. It bears repeating that if we are not yet ready to engage in such a practice, trying to let go of our rights prematurely can cause further fear, and we should stick with the practices of the mind and body given earlier.

But eventually we must come to this. For when we die, whether it be a physical death or the death of our self-concept, we will have to let go of everything we've been working for in our fear. All our efforts for personal happiness, all the striving for security, all the energy spent on avoiding catastrophes and the search for self-preservation—it will all have to go in the end.

Let us give this up now and not wait, so that we may be free to enjoy life without such oppression! Let us give up the fear associated with trying to protect ourselves, whether through making money, pleasing others, worrying about attack, and so on. Certainly, these efforts can be engaged as a support for our path. But when we come from too much care and worry, fearing for the survival of our self-concept, we kill off our true Selves in the process. When we devote ourselves to protecting our "freedom," we imprison ourselves in a lifetime of defensiveness.

When, by this strategy, are we supposed to be able to relax and enjoy the incredible bounty of life? This bounty is here and now, needing no defense and free for the asking. But we must let go of chasing our dreams and fearfully protecting our right to do so, trying to make things "work out" the way we say they should. In truth, we can't and don't have this right. We don't have the right to serve our "self" by our "self." For this self has become like an undisciplined child, requiring that we spend our lives in its demanding service.

Kahlil Gibran, in *The Prophet*, speaks to the futility of our never-ending efforts for security: "What shall tomorrow bring to the overprudent dog burying bones in the trackless sand as he follows the pilgrims to the holy city?" Let us stop giving so much attention to self-protection and self-glorification. Life is infinitely more powerful than we are anyway. We are not the omnipotent selves we think we are when attempting to defend against fear and change reality. Let us relax and flow with Life, no longer seeing it as that which would deprive us of what we need, but that which supports us in every detail when we but surrender to its Way.

We want to be glad for the feelings that come when our rights are taken away, our demand for self-importance shot down, our insistence on having things our way humbled. These are the causes of suffering, robbing us of our true right to be happy and free.

In giving up our false self, we claim our right to be real. We know ourselves to be whole, not needing reality to validate the illusions of who we are. And we sorely want to be free from the fear of such illusions being shattered, as life will surely do over and over again. We want to be free to plunge into life without so much concern for protection and security. We want to be free to love and connect deeply with people, without the fear of being rejected, free to soak up the variety of experience, to be outrageous in the expression of who we are, to recapture our innocence and the simplicity of Joy.

I remember well a particularly intense part of my own process where, during a period of tremendous change, loss of my old identities and attachments, I was unable to sleep for long stretches of time. There in the midst of my vulnerability, my defenses down, fear would visit me often in the night in all its splendor. Panicked about what the lack of sleep would mean, fantasies running wild without the grounding that comes with daylight, I was sure this was the beginning of the end. Without enough sleep, I would not be able to function through my exhaustion, responsibilities would get lost in the turmoil of my fog and confusion, and my health would fail. I cannot tell you the depth of my confrontation with utter powerlessness; there was nothing I could do to save myself.

Then, in the middle of the night, a favorite poem by Rumi came to mind: "Break the legs of what I want to happen. Humiliate my desire. Eat me like candy. It's spring, and finally I have no will." Recognizing fear for what it was, actually reveling in the energy of it, and making the connection to the fact that here, finally, I was experiencing the surrender I had always longed for, I began to laugh. Laugh with Joy, laugh with release. I was free and I was laughing. Nothing mattered; it didn't matter if I was exhausted, if everything failed, if the imaginary house of cards upon which I had built my idea of myself and my life crumbled. It was all made up! It simply wasn't real! There I lay, totally free, in the moment, to do whatever I wished. And I was laughing. To anyone outside it would have looked as though I had lost it and were fit for the madhouse. A fool for Freedom! A fool for Joy!

This is the power of giving up our rights.

## Sample

| Rights to Be Given Up | Reasons for Giving Them Up |
|---|---|
| 1. Anger at Alice for asking me to watch her daughter. | 1. This is an opportunity to take the attention off what "I want," to practice selflessness. I can discover the Joy of childlike innocence by spending time with her daughter. I can support my friend Alice in pursuing her dreams—this is part of what gives my life its meaning. |
| 2. Too much concern with making money at the expense of enjoying my life. | 2. Money is meant to be a support for enjoying my life; a servant, not a master. I want to be rich in Joy, soaking up the variety of life's experiences. To discover I don't need as much money will free me from so much tension and fear. |

| Rights to Be Given Up | Reasons for Giving Them Up |
|---|---|
| 3. Feeling guilty for saying "no" to John's request for my help. | 3. I don't have the right to make myself a victim of John's request; he simply asked for something. If it doesn't work for me to meet that request, if it would keep me from doing something I feel committed to, then saying no is a helpful response. I get to demonstrate to John that I'm living by my ideals, not selfishly, but out of my Vision. This is a gift to him. |

## Exercise 2: Active "Not-Doing"

It is perhaps easy to recognize some of the major fears of our lives. But the insidious, pervasive fears of everyday living have the cumulative effect of robbing us of our Joy. The constant, subtle tension of having to keep up with obligations, our daily maintenances, schedules, and responsibilities, seems to force us to sacrifice free choice for the demands of circumstance.

But we create all this as well! We have nothing but space and time, an open playing field to fill each moment as we choose. The forces of obligation which would compel us to give away our free choice must be put into their proper perspective. And this is our present exercise. Active "not-doing" is a powerful technique for standing quietly in the midst of fear's compulsions without responding. As we do so, the imagined threat disperses, leaving a spacious peace and the ability to choose our actions with freedom.

In active not-doing, we practice giving up our rights in the middle of trying to exercise them. We stop, no matter what is going on, and recognize the entitlement, the righteousness, the urge to "get" and "have" that is driving our actions. Standing quietly amid fear's storm, we give up this quest and face the consequences of letting go. We are then free to listen to Joy's direction instead, willing to change our course if it should prescribe something different.

Three times a day (or more if you are particularly eager for Joy) notice when you are on "automatic pilot," running around at the bequest of fear, busily getting things done. Notice especially when you feel the tension of fear that has you worry whether you will get something done the way you are "required" to, such as being on time, remembering to call someone, making sure the bills get paid, and so forth. Then, as you become aware of all this, stop, right in the middle of what you are doing, and refuse to move. Simply wait as the tension, the pressure, and the "commonsense" arguments of your fear try to impel you back into action. Wait even through the thought that says, "Okay, I've done this long enough; now let me rush back to what I was doing." Wait, with a quiet resolve not to have your life run by fear, until you *no longer have to move* and are willing to let go of the activity you were engaged in. Then, and only then, are you free to continue it as something that furthers your path to Joy, or to change your course, declaring yourself the master of your life, reclaiming a freedom you may have given up long ago.

Like Gandhi with the British Empire, we want to practice this "nonviolent noncooperation" with ourselves, declaring our independence from fear. You will be amazed at the incredible pull of your automatic drive to "get things done." Know the force of this as the force of fear and take heart in the idea that this is the very experience you were looking for when you decided to change your life. Indeed, it is the experience of changing the world, freeing it from fear. Every great leader or change maker has had to face just this pull.

Remember, too, that no amount of wishing can make illusions real, and recommit to your purpose with renewed intensity.

Once again, it is necessary to be wise in this. We don't want to stop in the middle of putting out a fire (that doesn't come until a later point in training!). Find those things that you are ready to let go of, standing at the edge of your comfort zones and remembering your commitment to Freedom. When you notice yourself being driven by a fear that you are not ready to let go of, remember that just the awareness that it is, in fact, fear which is calling the shots is a most important first step.

Let's look at the case of Susan, quoted earlier as saying that once she saw where her mind was running, she could brush away the little specks of fear. Here is her larger story, a good example of active not-doing and its ability to open up our path to healing.

## Susan

Susan was the oldest of five girls, looked up to with reverence by her sisters, a leader among the other children in the neighborhood. She was greatly rewarded for this leader-like character, and used it to compensate for the neglect she felt from her parents.

Then at age 11, her world turned upside down when her mother had a "nervous breakdown." Susan watched as her mother locked herself in the bathroom, threatening to kill herself, screaming wildly at her husband through the bathroom door. Then Susan's father broke down the door as paramedics came to take her mother away on a stretcher. Susan vividly remembers the crazed look on her mother's face, her disheveled hair, the way her eyes were "popping out of her head."

At that moment, Susan lost her innocence; the secure world she knew until that point was buried under a rockslide of pain, confusion, and disorientation. For a time, while her mother was in the hospital, she would sit in the middle of her bedroom floor wailing for hours upon end, waiting for her father to rescue her. He never did. He was too lost in his own pain, for which he compensated by "getting busy." Two of her siblings were sent away, and she lost the self-esteem of being their "big sister." The family was falling apart.

Finally, Susan found her solution: She watched her father running around busily and joined him. She would become the new mother in the house. She began cooking all the meals, cleaning and doing household chores, and making certain everyone's needs were taken care of.

Her father responded by scolding her for not doing these things more perfectly. This hooked her into trying harder and harder to do right by him. There was an unconscious agreement between them that they would play these roles in the interest of staying clear from their pain. They were busily engaged in building a new lifestyle to push away the old.

Susan became a compulsive "doer." In her marriage of later years, she found it impossible to stop and do nothing when I recommended it to her. Her experience, when she tried, was of a tremendous restlessness and agitation, the murmurings of her repressed anxiety churning below the surface.

In addition to her constant "doing," she made sure to wear a face of competence, someone who "had it all together" and could handle any situation. This, too, was a defense against the terrible fear of "becoming like her mother," that is, of decompensating and losing control.

These forces combined to form a repression which had her hiding her true feelings, her own needs for love and comfort, for being taken care of like an 11-year-old girl who had lost her mother (and father).

Our therapy was a matter of progressive invasions against this repression, with measured doses of exposure to the fear underneath, the memory of the incident at age 11. Her task was to become more and more conscious of the way in which she would "do" to avoid her fear, and then, simply, to tolerate "not doing." Insight into the source of her anxiety, the ability to connect her feelings to those of the 11-year-old, helped her to trust that it was safe to "not-do." She used this insight to remind herself that the threat of long ago was no longer present and she could afford to tolerate the feelings. She wanted desperately to be free, to relax in life, to fulfill her inner longing for an open exchange of love, rather than always having to earn love. When love was, in fact, offered, she would be too busy "doing" to receive or enjoy it, and would reactively set about trying to become worthy of it.

I will quote again the description, in Susan's own words, of her ultimate transformation. One day, as our therapy was progressing, she found herself in a meeting and wanted to contribute to the conversation. In her typical fashion, she began rehearsing a prepared speech to make it sound "interesting and important," as if to show her competence. Suddenly, she became aware of her hidden tactics. In catching herself, she had the opportunity to make a new choice, rather than being driven unconsciously by a choice made long ago. This was her experience in her own words:

> I could see where my mind was running. I was consciously noticing that I was afraid and [began] stepping back from my fear and letting myself be. And it was like I had an altered experience. I literally felt myself being lifted out of ego into some other plane and I started blissing out. I felt incredible love. I looked back at [my friend sitting next to me] and felt such love and harmony, and all the rest of it just fell away. [The fear] was like these little specks of dirt that you could just brush away, compared to this magnificent way, the "spirit" way, of looking at things.

This was the turning point for her. She had tasted freedom and there was no going back. Since that time, the painful experiences of her childhood have been allowed to surface and wash themselves out. She has resurrected the sense of innocence and safety she knew before her trauma. This innocence, integrated with her inherent leader-like power, has caused her to open up into a deeply loving person, someone who naturally attracts others who can reflect back this love.

## Exercise 3: Active "Not-Thinking"

As we resist physical action in active not-doing, we are simultaneously resisting the mental action which accompanies it. Therefore, it is equally valuable to practice such resistance through meditation, where we train our minds to stop in the middle of our thinking activity. This is giving up our right to think the thoughts of fear and separation.

In truth, it is giving up the right to think "our own" thoughts. For the thoughts we are familiar with are willful creations that would shape our perception to the reality we prefer. When we give these up, real "thoughts," thoughts of Joy and enduring Truth, fill our mind spontaneously. In fact, we have simply revealed what was always there behind the curtain of our dream images.

Begin a meditation practice, then, and notice how much your thoughts are devoted to the preservation of your "self." Our thinking mind is designed specifically to create the illusion of a separate self, a self which has the right to think up its own reality. Notice, too, how the thoughts generated by this self are built on fear, the fear of losing our individual identity and giving up its goals.

Let your meditation practice be a matter of noticing these thoughts and then actively "not-thinking" them, purposely letting them go and sitting in stillness. Check the impulse to engage new thoughts, "figure out" what is going on, and get back to the familiar mode of making your day happen. With each such impulse, simply notice the urge to pick up the thought and think it, and then relax back into stillness again.

If you are so inclined, find a book or take a workshop in a more formal meditation practice. Anything which promotes the ability to let go of thoughts will do the job. Ultimately, we want to practice noncooperation, not-doing, with our mental actions, just as we did with the physical actions of our daily lives. And again, remember that the thoughts of anger, guilt, boredom, and so on, are equally attempts to control reality. We want to give up our right to have these thoughts as well, finding and facing the fear behind them.

When we let go of our own thoughts, surrendering our "right" to think with a separate mind, "we," the separate self, will merge into Oneness. We will no longer know ourselves to be individuals in the strict sense, but will directly experience our participation in the whole. This is facing the core fear in its most universal sense, the surrender of our identity through thinking, our entire experience of separation, of individuality.

Without these thoughts, the separate mind is generating no activity to substantiate its existence. The dream of separation dissolves and the experience of Oneness returns to our minds.

Let us wait in the stillness, then, sitting in "pure consciousness," and know that a shift in perception *will* come. You may notice it first as a feeling of quiet, ease, relaxation, and not needing to control. The more you practice, the deeper your experience will be. And it will *do* you, taking you where you need to go, bringing up any fears that need to be faced along the way. Ultimately, its wisdom is such that it far transcends our ability to direct the path. Under its guidance, our journey to Joy can be greatly accelerated.

## Exercise 4: "Not-Doing" in Relationships

Here is a variation on active not-doing, to practice giving up the control we try to impose in our relationships. Using the techniques of psychodrama, re-create a scene where you had an argument or were upset with someone. Choose a situation that matters to you. With your partner(s), create the scene so that you can really feel your need to control, your fear of not winning the argument. See how it comes from your core fear. Then stop yourself, right in the middle of the argument, and just wait there, your need for control screaming at you, insisting that the other person is wrong! It's okay for it to scream; you want to be free. You want to have Joy, and ultimately, you want to be connected with the other person, not separated from him or her in fear.

Remember the question: "Would you rather be right or happy?" and just wait until the impulses pass. Simply sit with the frustration of not finishing your competition, leaving it undone. This is like the experience of leaving the world behind when you are ready to awaken. Experience the feeling of it, allow the power of that intensity, and resist the need, the voice of fear, which would compel you to do something about it, trying to force the other(s) to behave in the way you wish. Remember simply that this strategy has never worked and it never will. It's time to let go.

Before you start, tell the others involved what you will be doing and direct them to wait quietly as you stop yourself, supporting you in your goal by their silence. For more advanced practice, ask them to keep arguing, increasing the intensity and pitch as they try to reel you back in, subdue you, and make you feel wrong. And then, once again, see the madness for what it is. Put an end to the tired and painful dream of attack, defense, and more attack. By refusing to engage in the feast of fear, you will be setting yourself (and the others!) free.

## Exercise 5: Childlike Perception

This little exercise is a wonderful way to shift out of fear's perception. As we try to control reality, our awareness locks into a perception that shows only what is relevant to this goal. We pick out those features which help us to get what we want, pushing away the awareness of everything else. This leads to jaded perception, where the world becomes "ordinary," the beauty of things is lost, and we stop looking for Joy.

"Childlike perception" is an exercise for breaking out of this pattern, opening us up to the experience of the child, where everything is new and fresh, without the imposed meanings of our fear. It is also a very useful addition to active not-doing, helping us shake off the perspective of "having to get things done." Looking around at what is, instead of seeing only what we wish things were, we take off the blinders of our defensiveness, seeing the wonder of the present, the mysterious here-and-now.

Again, this exercise can be a useful addition to active not-doing, to be applied when you have stopped your activity and are standing in stillness. Or you can take it on whenever you want to tap into the timeless view, rediscovering the innocence of original perception. In the midst of your busy-ness, shake off the mind-set of fear by finding some object with many fine details. Move very close to this object, whether it is a rock or a tree trunk or the lines in your hand, and fix your attention on the details. Follow along the lines, the hills and valleys, very slowly and thoroughly. Invest yourself in the microcosmic view, discovering the world from a fresh perspective. If it helps, imagine yourself as a very tiny creature moving through the shapes and spaces, colors and shadows of this miniature world. You are reawakening the perception of the child, rediscovering innocent perception, perception not imposed upon by the restrictions of fear.

This passage from Dan Millman's *Way of the Peaceful Warrior* illustrates the experience:

"It's time to awaken your senses once again." I paused, digesting what he had said. "Again?" I asked. "Oh, yes. You once were bathed in brightness, and found pleasure in the simplest things." "Not recently, I'd venture." "No, not recently," he answered, taking my head in his hands, sending me back to my infancy.

My eyes open wide, staring intently at shapes and colors beneath my hands as I crawl on the tiled floor. I touch a rug and it touches me back. Everything is bright and alive.

I grasp a spoon in one tiny hand and bang it against a cup. The clinking noise delights my ears. I yell with power! Then I look up to see a skirt, billowing above me. I'm lifted up, and make cooing sounds. Bathed in my mother's scent, my body relaxes into hers, and I'm filled with bliss.

Some time later. Cool air touches my face as I crawl in a garden. Colorful flowers tower around me, and I'm surrounded by new smells. I tear one and bite it; my mouth is filled with a bitter message. I spit it out.

My mother comes. I hold out my hand to show her a wiggly black thing that tickles my hand. She reaches down and knocks it away. "Nasty spider!" she says. Then she holds a soft thing to my face; it talks to my nose. "Rose," she says, then makes the same noise again. "Rose." I look up at her, then around me, and drift again into the world of scented colors.

You can also practice this exercise as an eating meditation, paying attention to the subtle detail of the many sensations of the food you are eating, the sensations of the food touching all the various points of the inside of your mouth, of the subtle sting of the salivary glands releasing saliva, of the flavors erupting on your palate. Try combining this with active "not-doing," resisting the temptation to chew, guzzle, and swallow and just letting the food and its sensations play on your tongue.

And you can do this as a breathing meditation as well. Breathing is much like eating, where we ingest something from the environment and watch as it interpenetrates with our being. Notice the many "flavors" of the breath, of the world, which you are bringing inside you. Let the molecules of smell register on your receptors and dance. Drink up the particles of all-creation which have mingled with the air you are breathing. You might visualize, as did Teilhard de Chardin, that you are breathing in some of the same molecules that entered the bodies of Joan of Arc, of Martin Luther King, of Jesus or Gandhi or Moses. Then pour out your own creation with each exhale and send yourself out into the cosmos.

Notice, too, the many tiny sensations of the breath as it moves past the rim of your nose, causing the cilia inside your nose to sway in its wind, hitting the roof at the top of the nasal passages and traveling down the windpipe, causing the lungs to expand with their pressure and then moving through the alveoli into the bloodstream. You can almost feel this microscopic movement! And now you can journey through the incredible world of your body and take off with the same process.

If you are at first impatient with this exercise, know this is your fear trying to seduce you back into "business as usual." Stick with it, and after only a few minutes you will find yourself relaxing deeply, shifting your perception of what is important and remembering the Joy of discovering the world as if for the first time.

## Exercise 6: Rules for Making Choices

And now we take our practice to its completion. This exercise can bring us to the point of total freedom from undue care and worry, giving up the concern about whether reality will comply with our wishes. It can open us up to the transcendent perspective of the spirit in the moment-to-moment decisions of our lives.

These are the rules for making choices. They give the structure within which we apply all of our practices so far. They give the means by which we release fear in each choice we make, opening the doorway of the spirit into Freedom.

Since our goal is Joy, and whenever we are not wholly joyous we are in some way choosing or holding on to fear, then we want to become aware of how, moment-to-moment, we have been making such choices and bring them to consciousness. Again, even in choosing to go through our expected routine without reinventing our commitment in each moment, we are coming from the fear that says, "I must do so or else!"

Without fear, we will not suddenly become irresponsible. Rather, we will be free to choose our commitments, or satisfy the need of the moment in an even more effective way. And there will be no more cause to sacrifice our soul in the doing, for in our freedom from fear we choose that which nourishes the soul *and* fulfills our responsibilities.

These rules, then, are really a matter of asking in each moment what would serve Joy's purpose most effectively, and then listening for the answer without fear, paying attention to what is most appropriate and natural in the moment. This is our practice. Going through our day, we listen for Joy's direction, using the rules whenever we have a choice to make.

First, of course, we must become aware that we have been running on automatic, busily making choices according to a preordained agenda. This agenda, born of fear, is comprised of our best ideas for getting things done the way we think they should be done, working toward the reality of our wishes.

And even if we originally set the agenda according to Joy's direction, we must be willing to change our course moment-to-moment if Joy so directs. For our agendas must change even though our goal remains the same; only the form changes as Joy navigates through the fears we put in the way. We want to live, then, in an attitude of continual willingness, continual listening, continual letting go of our wishes and our rights.

This story makes the point nicely: A rabbi was walking to the synagogue one morning, as he did every day at the same time. On this particular morning, the policeman at the intersection was in an especially bad mood. He grumbled at the rabbi, "Where are you going today?" The rabbi, in all innocence, said, "I don't know." This was all the policeman needed to set him off. "What do you mean you don't know? Every morning at this time I watch you cross the street as you go to the synagogue. Are you trying to make trouble? Is that what you're doing? I'm taking you in to the station!" Later, at the police station, he asked the rabbi again, "Now, where were you going this morning?" The rabbi answered again, in all innocence, "I told you I didn't know. I thought I was going to the synagogue, but here I am at the police station!"

This is "living in the moment." In the movie *Being There*, the main character seems to be a simpleton, without all his faculties in order. Yet as the story unfolds, subtle miracles occur around the sense of presence he carries. One becomes swept up in the innocence with which he lives in the moment. Finally, at the end, he literally walks on water simply because, being in the moment, he had no thought that this was not possible. Perception shifted, circumstance gave way, and what was most appropriate to the moment was allowed to unfold.

And now for the rules.

## Rule 1—Face the Fears of Each Option

The only real rule, of course, is to find and face our fear, bypassing the chief defense and doing what the fear says not to. Sometimes, however, the fear to face is not immediately clear. Sometimes, we are not sure which of our options is coming from fear and which from Joy. "Should I take this job offer or that one?" "Should I go out with so-and-so or not?"

"Should I start this project now or later?" Whenever you are confronted with two or more possible options and are unsure which one opens the path to Joy, be willing to face the fears of each option fully. Live through in imagination (using "What happens next?" or "Embracing the fear," for example) the full implications of each choice until you are completely willing to go down each of the paths. Having no investment in a particular outcome, your perception will shift and the "right" choice will become clear. You will become available to seeing what serves Joy best.

### Rule 2—Face the Fear of Making the Wrong Choice

Sometimes, it may still seem that more than one choice is equally valid. In this case, look for the fear that says, "I had better make the right choice or else . . . ," and be willing to face the fear of making the *wrong* choice. Again, with this you will be free of secret investment, willing to "hear" whatever is most appropriate for the fulfillment of the situation.

### Rule 3—Making Any Choice Is Better Than No Choice

Sometimes, too, the fear to face is simply the fear of making a choice at all. We can too easily become immobilized, thinking we must be exact in our listening for Joy. Another way, then, to face the fear of making the wrong choice is to know that making *any* choice is better than making no choice. At least we want to make the choice not to choose right now so that we are committed to a direction and are moving forward along its path. With this, we will learn from whatever option we choose. In fact, when we have been paralyzed with indecision, it can be a most potent learning experience to have forged ahead through fear and committed to a course of action.

Of course it is necessary to gather information before making a choice. But after a point, when we have as much information as can be reasonably expected, to wait any longer in the hope that something new will show up is to avoid the fear of accepting reality-as-it-is. We create more pain for ourselves this way than either choice would bring, the pain of not moving forward with our lives.

If it is helpful, know that "all roads lead to Rome" or "Home," so in a very real sense there is no "wrong" choice. The goal is to be without fear, not to make the "right" choice. Therefore, it doesn't matter so much *what* you choose, but *that* you choose and get into action facing fears and finding Joy.

### Rule 4—Take Yourself at Your Level of Readiness

Sometimes, however, it is not wise to release our defenses too quickly. it may be necessary to face our fear in measured doses, checking out whether we feel safe enough to proceed to the next step before plunging in. Another important rule, therefore, is to take yourself at the level at which you are ready. Do not try to let go of fear until the promise of Joy is stronger than the threat of fear. As we have mentioned, it can be but further fear that says, "I must get to Joy immediately." The job at this point is to face the fear you are ready to face, perhaps even the fear of not getting to Joy immediately.

### Rule 5—Set Boundaries as Necessary

If you are not ready to face a certain fear, then set up the boundaries you need in order to feel safe first. If, for example, we are angry and are just unable to transform it, then we must first understand what it is we are afraid of, setting up the boundaries within which we can feel safe from the fear. Anger is a fear-based attempt to set up such boundaries. It is the attempt to protect oneself, forcibly, from that which is threatening. It also serves (we hope) to make the other feel guilty enough that he will stop scaring us. Instead of this, let us admit that we are scared and set up boundaries in a conscious way. In taking care of our need to feel safer, we may let go of trying to control with our anger. Once these boundaries are established, then we may begin to work through the fear behind the anger.

Running away from fear, whether through denial, separation, or even dissociation, is similarly an attempt to set up boundaries for safety. In working with a patient with Dissociative Identity Disorder (formerly called Multiple Personality Disorder), I learned how necessary her dissociation was for the sake of mere survival. As a child subject to horrendous abuses, there was, of course, no way she could practice "facing her fears." And so she would split off into many selves, putting herself into a picture on the wall, becoming a "boss" who could exercise some authority, or becoming pure spirit without a body at all. Only this made it possible for her to survive so that at some later point she might have the chance to reintegrate into a sense of wholeness again, facing the fears one at a time that would make that possible.

Therefore, if our fear is great enough, it can be wise and necessary to get some distance from it so that we may regroup, building our readiness to work it through. Once we have enough experience with setting boundaries, we will come to trust in our safety, discovering that the fear cannot force us to react defensively. We know that nothing can invade our boundaries, or better, nothing can truly threaten us. The boundaries then become unnecessary. The walls come tumbling down in a natural and joyous way, and we are then free to join with that which we were protecting ourselves from.

## Rule 6—Be Willing to Give Up What You Thought You Wanted

The promise that facing our fear will show us it is not real does not mean that we get everything the way we want. As we have seen, we will not experience freedom from fear until we are willing to give up this compulsion. Our next rule, then, is that in order to experience Joy, we have to be willing to give up what we *thought* we wanted, to discover that Joy fills the need infinitely better.

Facing the fear of letting these things go will never take away our sense of integrity and wholeness, but only add to it. Indeed, living under fear's dictate, while it promises to keep us safe, exacts a far greater toll upon our psyche, spirit, and body than does facing fear. If we want healing, we have to become more interested in the freedom from fear that comes with knowing that nothing can destroy our wholeness, than in holding on to our old ideas of what will keep us safe.

## Rule 7—Remember: Nothing Matters More Than Joy

If the ultimate fear is that of giving up the separation and returning to Oneness, then the many fears of our lives are but different versions of this loss of our individual identity. Let us label this the fear of "death." We believe that death will take away everything we have "dreamed" of. This is true, we believe, for the death of our body as well as the little deaths of every day.

We, therefore, want to actively take on the fear of death, to expose this final saboteur for the illusion it truly is. If fear is built on the idea that something is threatening to take away our feeling of safety and wholeness, then facing and "living through" such fear shows us that something in us has survived—we are still whole and intact. And if we are experiencing this wholeness, we are indeed still safe.

Each survival of the minideaths of everyday life prepares us for the great death where we let go of the physical body. And in surviving our fear of this death we are truly free. The spirit quietly and naturally expands into peace with ourselves and with all things. As Emmanuel, a spiritual teacher once said, "The one thing to know about death . . . it's perfectly safe!"

Living through the fear of death shows us, once on the other side, that it was not the be-all and end-all we have always imagined. Indeed it is but another opening into Truth, as Kahlil Gibran writes so beautifully in *The Prophet:* "For what is it to die but to stand naked in the wind and melt into the sun? And what is it to cease breathing, but to free the breath from its restless tides, that it may rise and expand and seek God unencumbered?"

The final rule, then, is to remember that nothing matters to us more than Joy, not even the survival of our individual self. Joy is more important to us than comfort, than "feeling good," than getting enough sleep or avoiding problems. It is more important than making money, having security and protecting our investments. And yes, it is more important than "self-preservation." It is what we are trying to preserve ourselves for.

As we are confronted with the many choices of every day and the major choices of our lifetime, we want to practice with this attitude of "Nothing matters to me more than Freedom and Joy, and I am willing, in each moment, to let everything go." We want to practice accepting that, in truth, we have no control over reality. We are utterly powerless to make things "turn out" as we wish. But so, too, are we released from the responsibility of trying to do so, knowing we cannot succeed. Nothing, then, owns us—we are free. With this, we may rebuild our world anew, fresh, in each moment, never again sacrificing our Joy for the sake of old and stale ideas of how things should be. This is the attitude that should be at the bedrock of our practice, this is the attitude that will keep our practice pure, and this is the attitude that will ensure our return to Joy.

# PART III

# LIVING YOUR VISION

# AWAKENING YOUR POTENTIAL FOR BEING FULLY ALIVE

Our journey together so far has taken us to a place of great promise, potential freedom, and the clear view of Joy. Three "doorways to consciousness" have been explored: (1) the doorway of the mind—reinventing thought and perception, (2) the doorway of the body—releasing physically stored blockages, and (3) the doorway of the spirit—ascending through to a higher perspective. Each of these provides access to the other two, and any path of growth requires that all three be resolved together.

But it is not enough simply to know the tools for releasing fear; this is not yet radical Joy. True fulfillment is more than managing or even freeing ourselves from problems and then maintaining a status quo. Our spirit begs for full self-expression. After the resolution of fear we must ask, "What now do I do? What is the meaning of my life?"

We have seen how fear has masterminded our strategy for living, how it has stolen our Joy. We have learned as well how to dismantle its foundation. Now we must design a new structure for our lives. With the release of fear, the healing of our relationship with reality, and the discovery of our true Self, there is a natural extension of Joy that must be expressed, reaching out to become actualized in the world. This is the call to live our Vision, and we must give ourselves to it fully if we are to realize our Joy.

When Mother Teresa received her calling, the Vision of her soul's purpose, she asked permission to leave the abbey where she was teaching and went, with no preparation or securities, to the streets of Calcutta. She wanted to give her life to helping "the poorest of the poor." When she got off the train, she had nothing but her Vision—no plans and no provisions. She didn't even know where she would stay that night.

The first person she saw lying in the street was a man who was dying. Mostly skin and bones, he was infested with lice and smelled so bad that no one wanted to get near him. Mother Teresa went up to him and, in an act of utter simplicity, started cleaning him. When the man, so weak he could barely lift his head, asked her "Why are you doing this?" she answered, "Because I love you." This was the birth of her philosophy of "love in action," simply moving to meet the need of the moment according to one's high Ideal. She was able to let go of her fear, accept reality as it was, and act in pure and selfless love.

Radical Joy comes from living a life of full self-expression, finding one's purpose and giving all of oneself to it. When we release ourselves from the shackles of fear, the Life Impulse is free to express itself through us, without impediment. Years later, Mother Teresa explained that if she hadn't helped that one person in the beginning, none of the countless others she and her sisters have helped would have been served. The Vision manifests from a single first step. Setting our intention clearly from the start, obstacles become opportunities for reaching our destination, and nothing can stand in the way of Joy's expression.

Our prescription for Vision building includes three steps: First, we find and face our fear, watching its illusion of reality dissolve and clear the way for Joy. Next, sitting in "pure consciousness" (consciousness that is unobstructed by fear), we wait and "listen" for what is appropriate in the way of action, allowing our Joy to direct how it wants to be expressed. Finally, we set our goals and act, building our Vision one step at a time.

The first step has been the focus of our work so far. Where we might be tempted to think we are "healed" at this point, ready to rush forth into action, we must be wise to the subtleties of fear and watch for its tendency to sneak back in. We want to tend lovingly to our new freedom and nurture it into maturity. This means being willing to take no action, if indeed it is our fear that is compelling us to rush in and "fix" the world (the familiar mistake of trying to force reality to comply with our wishes) or to create an agenda from our past experience, rather than letting something completely new appear, something unrecognizable to our fear-based conditioning.

This is where the second step comes in: sitting in "pure consciousness" and waiting for the Impulse-to-Joy to direct us. Such a practice necessitates that this Impulse is not drowned out by the noise of fear. And as we have seen, the key to this is to relinquish our investment in having circumstances turn out in a particular way. With "a little willingness," the willingness to give up our old ways because we want to find our fulfillment, we can ask of the Impulse-to-Joy what it would have us do. The only thing keeping us from asking this and knowing our answer is a continuing fear thought: "What if the answer doesn't come through, or what if it isn't accurate? What if the answer doesn't handle things the way *I* want them handled?," and so forth. Each of these fears needs to be let go, to clear our altar and invite in Joy's direction.

The third point—setting our goals and taking action—is

192 LIVING YOUR VISION

not really about making plans, usually a fear-driven act that seeks security and control over the future. Instead, it is about recognizing Joy's prompting and committing to it with a full intention to act. In staying attentive to this commitment, we recognize when our goals need to be changed in the interest of fulfilling our purposes most effectively. But goals provide the necessary structure for taking whatever action is called for in the moment. We are to "step back" and follow the Impulse-to-Joy. This is not a passive maneuver; we do not step back and meditate our lives away. Following Joy's lead, we set our goals and take action to realize our Vision of a world transformed. We have work to do.

There is another advantage to setting our goal from the start. With our sights firmly set, all obstacles that would attempt to throw us off course become opportunities for redirecting toward our predetermined goal. Indeed, we can use the obstacles to help us achieve our goal. Nothing will deter us if the goal is set and we stay true to our commitment, refusing to let fear back in. As Joseph Campbell said in *The Power of Myth*, if you "follow your bliss you put yourself on a kind of track that has been there all the while, waiting for you, and the life that you ought to be living is the one you are living. When you can see that, you begin to meet people who are in the field of your bliss, and they open the doors to you. I say, follow your bliss and don't be afraid, and doors will open where you didn't know they are going to be."

And so we begin now to build, not just a strategy for living, but a direction for our lives, something which will define who we are and how we are to be in the world in a new way, for the radical fulfillment of Joy.

# CHAPTER 7

## VISION QUESTING

This is the true joy in life, the being used for a purpose
recognized by yourself as a mighty one, the being a
force of nature instead of a feverish selfish little clod of
ailments and grievances complaining that the world
will not devote itself to making me happy.

I am of the opinion that my life belongs to the whole
community and, as long as I live, it is my privilege to
do for it whatever I can. I want to be thoroughly used
up when I die, for the harder I work, the more I live.

I rejoice in life for its own sake. Life is no brief candle
to me. It is a sort of splendid torch which I've got to
hold up for a moment and I want to make it burn as
brightly as possible before handing it on to future
generations.

—George Bernard Shaw, *Man and Superman*

When the Native Americans went on a Vision Quest, they
took with them nothing but a blanket. They wore no clothes,
brought no food or water, built no shelter. They would simply
dig a hole in the earth, declaring their oneness with the Great
Mother from which they came, and fast, for up to four days,
while "begging" for a Vision.

These rigors provided an effective if not challenging
method of releasing one's defenses and finding a greater Truth
waiting on the other side. Our approach has been similar. For
in understanding and taking action against our fears, we, too,
have been practicing the release of defenses in the service of
finding our Joy. Now it is time for the harvest. It is time to
receive our Vision.

One's Vision is one's highest Ideal. It is the picture of
Fulfillment that informs our perception and guides our actions

in every detail of living. It is that which gives birth to our new identity, sculpting and defining it with each step we take toward the realization of our dreams. When the Vision is fulfilled, our true Self is fully expressed and nothing is left wanting.

The discovery of Vision arises spontaneously with the release of fears, for the Joy that emerges in this release wants to be expressed in action. Such action gives our life its meaning, purpose, and direction. We might say that freeing ourselves from fear enables us to "hear" our Vision, as it speaks to us about what wants to happen, how circumstances naturally want to work together, for our greatest Good. Without fear's need to force circumstances into the pigeonholes of our preferences, we are free simply to follow the flow of where things want to move, what is appropriate and natural, what is harmonious. We have relinquished our judgments of what is "good" and "bad," of what serves our individual desires and what does not. Instead we stand in the place of witness-on-high, simply observing what makes for true fulfillment. Having let go the need for reality to conform to our wishes, we are unattached to a particular answer, willing and available to hear whatever Vision is prescribed by reality-as-it-is.

One's Vision, then, is that which serves Joy, that which fulfills the higher Truth. It is the action component of Joy, the prescription for how the Joy of the Spirit wants to manifest in the world of form. And such action is devoted to transforming suffering, releasing the fears which block the recognition of Joy, so that the world may return to its original state of Oneness.

## Sitting in Pure Consciousness

As we begin our Vision quest, a most crucial question arises: If all our decisions in the past were driven by the core fear and chief defense, how do we decide on a Vision without these tools, and how can we know the decision is not further fear and defensiveness in disguise? We have said that the Vision actually shows up by itself, spontaneously, once we have released our fears and are free to discover it. So the question should really be "How do we discover the decision?" rather than "How do we decide?" This point is so important that we must explore it fully. We don't want to run the risk of distorting our Vision with old defenses and fears, imposing ourselves on others with the secret wish to have them conform to our will.

The answer to our question involves the practice of what we will call "sitting in pure consciousness." Pure consciousness is consciousness that is still, free and clear of the frenetic thoughts inspired by fear. With respect to Vision questing, this means "not knowing" in advance what our Vision should be. To achieve this, we must find and release the fears that would have us predetermine what the "right" Vision is for us, the Vision we *want* to hear.

Once in this state of pure consciousness, we then "listen" for the what-to-do, paying attention to what is called for, without attachment to a particular answer. This sitting in pure consciousness is a critical step in Vision questing. We do not want to use our old devices for deciding what our vision should be; that would simply give us more of what we always had. Instead, we want to catch this very impulse as it tries to arise and then resist it, finding and facing the fear behind it. In resisting the impulse, we become willing to sit without knowing what to do at all. Then, free of fear and hidden investment, the awareness of what is appropriate becomes clear, unobstructed by self-serving agendas.

When we no longer need to hear a particular answer, we experience a great release from the need to protect and defend, to struggle against external threats, to grasp at our wants and be devastated when we fail. This release in itself brings Joy and shows us what we were not willing to see before. It shows us what we have always known would be appropriate and necessary for Joy, but were too afraid or defended against to recognize. It is simply a matter of what serves the higher Good, what makes things work effectively, and what is our part in helping to accomplish this. Without our controlling ideas of how things *should* work, there is nothing to interfere with the awareness of how they *do* work: reality-as-it-is.

## Pitfalls and Guidelines on the Path to Vision

Sitting in pure consciousness, without the adulteration of fear and defense, gives a deep experience of Freedom. We may be tempted to interpret this as the freedom from needing to do anything. Without fear, we no longer have the need to fix or change reality, and may wish simply to rest in our Freedom, observing the "play of consciousness," the dance of energy and form. Or we may wish to enjoy our Freedom by doing whatever we please, understanding that there is nothing to fear from the consequences of such action.

Both of these responses fail to recognize our infinite interconnectedness with others and the effects of our "individual" actions on the whole. To come to the point of Freedom and rest in it by ourselves, "sitting on the mountaintop" and playing "above it all," is not true Freedom and cannot bring true Joy. It is still fear in the form of "self"-ishness, the separated identity that does not yet recognize its Oneness with all of creation. We literally cannot be fully released until everything is released with us. The Buddha, upon the moment of his Enlightenment, looked around in amazement and said, "Isn't it wonderful? Isn't it marvelous? All sentient beings awaken together!" This is the return to Oneness, wherein we recognize our interdependency and realize that we must help release others into Joy if we ourselves are to be released.

When listening for Vision, then, another point to consider is this: How does the Joy I feel want to be expressed in a way where others are released into Joy as well? This is the service aspect of Vision questing—it is called "seva" in Sanskrit, or "bakhti yoga" in Hinduism. Selfless service, devotion to others, can be a complete path to realization by itself. In the Ramayana epic, this ideal is represented in the form of Hanuman, the monkey god who served Lord Rama. He is often depicted as ripping open his chest to expose the love of his heart. And Mother Teresa's Missionaries of Charity devote themselves tirelessly to serving the poorest of the poor, or "Jesus in His distressing disguise." Similarly, the bodhisattva is one who has taken a vow to continue on the wheel of death and rebirth, postponing personal Enlightenment until each "sentient being," even every blade of grass, is also enlightened.

To rest in the experience of Freedom amid a world which begs for healing is to stay defended against the fear of taking action! There is work to be done, and our release from fear means nothing if it does not make a difference in the world. How does this Freedom want to be translated, such that you experience the Joy of releasing others into Freedom? How does it want to be fulfilled such that the world may find its Joy right in the middle of the human condition? Certainly, our Vision is to be that which is inspiring to us, that which captures the essence of Joy for us to celebrate, but for this to be possible it must include Joy for others as well. After all, we want to live in a world where even the possibility of the pain we have experienced is erased, and everyone we see is safe and healed, so that we may feel safe and healed in their presence, too.

Along with this is an additional important point in the process of Vision questing: "If my path up to now has been driven by fear and defense, should I not abandon it entirely and start anew? Is a radical lifestyle change not necessary?" The answer, again, requires that we sit in pure consciousness, not deciding on an answer in advance. We want to practice not knowing but listening, not deciding but inquiring. And the fears and defenses which would obscure the answer must be released: Are we afraid to make such a radical change? Are we, on the other hand, more afraid not to? Is the impulse to escape our past—with its pain, fear, and limitation—a defensive attempt to reach for personal joy, a denial of responsibilities? Is there, alternatively, a desire to cling to our familiar lifestyle, avoiding a radical change out of fear of the unknown, the fear of giving up security?

Here, too, we are to find and face our fears so that we may discover what is most appropriate in the way of lifestyle change. We must be completely willing to stay in our present circumstances and at the same time be completely willing to make a radical change in order for our Vision to show up. Only with this willingness will we be free of the investment in outcomes that would keep us from knowing what serves the higher Purpose.

## The Training Arena for Vision

With this kind of willingness, we discover a most astonishing revelation: The path we have taken in our lives, with all of its pain and Joy, disappointment and fulfillment, has been the perfect breeding ground for our Vision. The many experiences that have brought us to where we are right now have groomed us precisely to release fear and express Joy in our own unique way. We have built our entire identity on this path and this identity is not to be thrown away. Rather, it is to be released from its fear and used in the service of what is highest and finest in us. Everything we've been devoted to, everything we've been struggling with, has become our training arena, our schoolroom. No one is more intimately experienced with the perspective given by our path than we are. And now that we are healing, no one is better able to harness its potential for healing others than we are. We are exquisitely poised to express this potential.

To explore this further, our fear-defense dynamic is the thing we have most wanted to transform about the world, the thing we have been most devoted to healing, most interested in mastering. We have become intimately familiar with its ways, with the struggle against it, with the frustrated search for Joy that sprang from it. Again, we have been uniquely groomed to discover the way out of its prison and have found our identity in the release from it. We now want to enjoy our freedom by dismantling its walls and creating a world in which it can never be rebuilt.

Our chief defense has been our best way to try to accomplish this and it has, perhaps, produced some successes in life. But notice that these successes have always come at the great cost of keeping us feeling as if it is never enough. We can never "arrive" and enjoy the fruits of our labors because the fear which motivated the effort was always present, ready to pounce if we should let up even for a moment. We would work harder and harder to defend against it, trying to reach the point where we could be sure the fear would never strike. Of course, in using our defense we kept the fear alive by creating something to defend against. Therefore, we have set it up that we can never be completely successful.

In Vision questing, we work toward the same goal with the opposite strategy: Instead of running away from fear by exercising our defense, we go straight into it to find real Joy and create true safety. "In my defenselessness my safety lies" *A Course in Miracles* tells us. "Strength through softness," the Tai Chi masters say. We use our experience with fear and defense to teach and practice what it is to be free of the suffering they created. This is how we find our own Joy. This is how we help others to find theirs.

## Vision as the Healing of Fear

Our vision comes as one of two possible responses to this. Upon letting go of defensiveness and finding freedom from fear, we often become impelled to help others do the same. Knowing the ins and outs of this dynamic so well, we have become identified with the process of releasing it. We find our Vision in this process, fulfilling ourselves by helping others release their own fear-defense dynamic. Knowing the suffering that it can cause, we want to build a world which is free from its effects.

The alternative response is to discover that we no longer want to devote ourselves to the goals we were trying to accomplish before. We let go our attachments and pursue a new course. We begin to build a world that is the opposite of the life we knew under the reign of fear. Free from the bonds of our past, the many possibilities previously closed off to us beg to be explored. One's Vision can become a matter of expressing the talents and potentials previously suppressed by the preoccupation with fear. Remember the woman who was trained out of being an artist by her parents at a young age, and then covered the floor with beautiful drawings once freed from this training? If we have built a defense as a survival technique and survival is no longer an issue, then we are free to really live and soak up what is meaningful and joyous about life.

St. Francis, at the beginning of his spiritual career, had a death-rebirth experience. Having come back from the war with "fevers," he would go into a state of delirium and move into an ecstasy with God. Experiencing a freedom from any sense of lack or deprivation, he saw the futility of a life lived for security. Not knowing how to translate this into a vocation that would "work" in the world, he began recklessly trying to cast off his and others' possessions. His father, deeply entrenched in materialism, became furious. Confronting Francis, he demanded that his son show respect for his father. Francis replied compassionately, "I'm not your son anymore." He stripped off his clothes, returning them and his name to his father, and walked out of the town square naked, "born again," to start his life anew.

His desire was to become "like a beggar," in the image of Christ. As a beggar, he could be free from the entrapment of material concerns and "loveless toil." He could be free to express the Impulse-to-Joy and help others do the same. This was the beginning of his Vision to help people get past the encumbrances of materiality and back to the simplicity of loving God. At one point, he likened his Vision to that of the larks, simple creatures who need only a few berries and a sip of water to sing in praise of the Creator and fly up to the heavens. He would express his Joy wherever it was welcomed, even to a tree full of birds who, twittering loudly as he approached, fell silent while he sermonized to them, and then began singing noisily once again upon his completion.

Francis's Vision was so passionate because it was motivated by an experience of what he knew did not work. He had been raised with material comforts, and lived a life of self-interested gratification. Upon his transformation he saw the pointlessness, and in fact the trap, of all this. Such an insight became the vehicle for his message.

Gandhi helped a man find his Vision in a similar way. This man, a Muslim, had been fighting with bitter hatred against the Hindus, in vengeance for his 6-year-old son's death at the hands of a Hindu. Gandhi was immersed in a fast which had him close to death, in protest of such fighting. This Muslim was now helplessly torn between his love for the Mahatma and his need for revenge. He rushed toward Gandhi and threw some food at him, demanding that Gandhi eat so he would not have his death on his conscience. Gandhi asked what was the source of his hatred for the Hindus. The man told him about his son and added, "And now I live in hell." Joining with this man, Gandhi said quietly, "I know a way out of hell. Find a little boy, about 6 years old, whose parents have been killed in this war, and raise him as your own. Only make certain that he is a Hindu boy." This man would find his freedom from hell by walking straight into the heart of his fear, transforming the very things which caused his pain into a Vision for healing.

## Lori

When I first met Lori, she was already confined to a wheel-chair with advanced multiple sclerosis. She came to see me because she wanted to make sure she didn't end up living a meaningless life. Her life, in fact, had been full of accomplishment, but she felt restless inside, as if she had been occupying herself with busy-ness.

In our first session I told her that I thought she was "fierce" in a good way. Fierce in her determination not to let her disease stop her. Fierce in her resolve to stand up for her rights and the rights of others. One of her many accomplishments included her work as an advocate for people with disabilities. She wanted to make sure they didn't get stopped by their limitations, and that the law would provide for their equal rights. This, in itself, was a wonderful Vision. Still, she was restless and something inside her felt unresolved.

In working together we discovered the core fear and chief defense behind her strategy for living—she *had* to find her meaning, or else! She was busy "accomplishing" her life away, with all of her fierceness, never free to enjoy the fruits of her efforts. She had a fear of standing still and a constant feeling of "it's never enough." As a result, she was driving herself in unhealthy ways, ending up drained and unfulfilled.

In time, she learned to face this fear by "not-doing" and "not being productive." At first, this was extraordinarily difficult for her as feelings of "I'm wasting my life . . . I'm going to wither away into nothing" tried to seduce her back into action. But eventually her defense broke and she came to realize that the greatest influence she could have on others, the most meaningful accomplishment, would be to find her own peace, free from the fear of having to accomplish and defend.

In so doing, she would be giving others the message that they didn't have to work so hard either. She began following a particular suggestion that the way to have peace is to teach peace, thereby discovering it must be in us in order to be able to teach it. She still works as an advocate for people with disabilities, but has included herself as one of those people who need to be taken care of. In a recent session, she announced with some surprise, "I'm actually accomplishing more now, but it feels different. It's not like it's coming from me, and so I don't feel drained or restless. It just flows now."

## Veronica

Veronica was a holistic nurse by trade. At 46 years old she carried a constant worry, on her face and in her voice, the signs of an anxiety that had shaped her personality throughout a lifetime.

Exploring the source of this, I learned that she had indeed been raised in an atmosphere of great anxiety from the time she was 18 months old. It was then that her mother died of a brain aneurysm, slumping over Veronica's crib as she was picking her up. After this, her father married a severely abusive woman. He began drinking for solace and became violent. Veronica started dating at an early age to escape the scene at home and was date-raped at age seventeen. As awful as this man was, she married him to "get away." He had a series of affairs, which he flaunted in front of her, coming home in between women to beat her physically and mentally.

One day in session with me, Veronica related a dream she had had the night before. In the dream, she was very young and sitting on the floor of a large car. Her favorite gerbil was balanced on the frame of the half-open window of the car. She watched as the gerbil fell into the car and "died." As if in slow motion, she reached up to push it back onto the window frame. With this, the gerbil came back to life, only to fall in and die again. Once more, Veronica pushed it back up to revive it. This went on repeatedly until she awoke.

I asked her if this scene reminded her of anything. When

she drew a blank, I gently provided the thought, "Didn't your mother 'fall in' over a ledge like that when she died in front of you?" With this, Veronica had a full-blown recall of the memory of her mother's death, buried under a lifetime of repression and anxiety, with all the affect of an 18-month-old little girl. Finally becoming still, she realized she had wanted to push her mother back up over the crib to bring her back to life, but was too little at the time to do so. She had been suffering from this feeling of inadequacy and helplessness ever since. (Interestingly, the morning after her dream, she awoke and found her gerbil had, in fact, died in the night. She considered the dream a gift from her pet.)

Veronica grew much quieter inside herself as a result of this session. Years of anxiety had been relieved simply by virtue of this insight. Shortly after, however, she came into a session full of anger. She was beginning a relationship with someone who, for the first time, was treating her with appropriate respect and love. Recounting the abuses she had suffered throughout the years, she banged out her feelings on the pillow so as not to sabotage this new relationship with old expectations of abuse. At the peak of her release she declared with fury, "No one is going to hurt me again!" The shift in energy patterns fully visible on her face let me know that she had broken the back of the anxiety. She was now able to contact the strength which had carried her through all of her traumas, this time without the anchor of her fear to weigh her down.

It was the next week that she found her Vision. She came into my office with a knowing look and said, "I now know what I'm going to do with the rest of my life—I want to open a practice in holistic healing for heart disease." Answering the question on my face, she said, "You see, I know what it is to have a broken heart; mine's been broken every which way but loose. That's why I went into nursing, without realizing it. I wanted to heal broken hearts!" She had transformed her pain into a most meaningful expression of the lessons she had

earned, turning her own suffering into healing and offering
t to others.

## Accepting the Vision

Vision, then, often comes as a response to freedom from
the fears of the past. But remember, too, that in listening for
Vision we may discover that we are asked to do the same work,
or some variation thereof, we were involved in before. The
old Zen saying is relevant here: "What did you do before
Enlightenment?" "Chopped wood, carried water." "And what
did you do after Enlightenment?" "Chopped wood, carried
water." But what a difference in the way we chop wood and
carry water!

It is not necessary to envision a radically different lifestyle
or change of circumstances. If this is called for, it must be
with the clear awareness that it serves the higher Good, not
our personal wishes. If, on the other hand, we are to stay put,
perhaps in a less glamorous, less romantic role than we had
hoped for, let it be with the same clarity of awareness that
communicates to others more powerfully than any single
action can. As Mother Teresa said, "If God puts you in a
palace, accept it, accept it, accept it. If he puts you on the
streets of Calcutta, accept it, accept it, accept it." Radical shift
or no, we must certainly make the inward shift from fear to
Joy, working with the very dreams and motivations we have
nurtured our entire lives, but with freedom from any need to
defend them.

Above all, we are not to let go or deny these dreams—their
source is the Impulse-to-Joy, and while our approach to trying
to fulfill them has been fear-inspired and therefore painful,
they are our heart's longing still. Do not make the mistake of
considering your past a waste, something to be escaped—it
has been the perfect training ground to discover what does
and does not work to live a life of Joy. It has brought you to

the point where you now can understand just how your fears and defenses have been driving you and how you want to transform your relationship with them.

Remember, you have been uniquely groomed by your particular life path to actualize the lessons you've learned for the good of all. Everything you have gone through has served to bring you to where you are now. All that is needful is to let go of the fear that says it must happen in the way you dictate, for you cannot tolerate the alternative. It is this that puts the blinders on so we cannot see the way to *allow* it to happen and come to fruition.

Vision comes from a higher Source. Letting go of our personal will, infinite opportunities show up for the fulfillment of true Purpose, opportunities which had always been there but were invisible while we wore the blinders of fear. Taking off these blinders, we can see clearly once again. The view is vast and broad, encompassing all of creation, and pointing the way for us to walk to Fulfillment, taking our right place in the grand scheme of things. This is the Vision of a world returned to Oneness. This is the answer to our heart's longing. This is the Joy we have always remembered, and have found again at last.

## EXERCISES

The exercises for finding our Vision are designed to help us attune to what is actually the most natural of impulses— to act in accord with the universal flow of things. To accomplish this, we will review the life journey once again. This time, it will be used to gain insight into the leanings and inclinations of our soul. Although it contained the hidden agenda of fear, our path has been motivated at every turn by the soul's urging toward Joy. Our successes and our failures have trained us to fulfill a specific task that no one else can. We know the pitfalls and subterfuges of fear that come up as we reach for the particular expression of Joy we have been attempting to live.

In reviewing our life journey we will move through three exercises. First, we will recapture the innocence of childhood. Next, we will examine how the core fear and chief defense altered our course through life. And finally, having freed ourselves from the rut of the fear-defense habit, we will go to the scene of our highest Vision fulfilled, where we have realized ourselves fully and are living a life of radical Joy.

## Exercise 1: Recapturing the Innocence of Childhood

To begin, we remember the childlike innocence we once knew, before our core fear and chief defense were created. This is the state we have been trying to recapture in using the chief defense, protecting ourselves from the fear which threatened to take the experience away. Who were you before this fear, before such protection was necessary? Who were you in this state of carefree innocence, where even the idea of threat was inconceivable? Let us go back to this time, fully immersing ourselves in what it was like then. We will do a meditation now, bringing this experience to life again, evoking the sense of Joy that is possible only when fear is gone from our minds. Again, you may want to tape-record this meditation in advance, to let yourself fully relax into the experience without having to read at the same time.

If you can't remember your childhood, then tap into the archetypal memory, the collective picture of childhood innocence. We all know what this is supposed to be like. If thinking about your childhood triggers anxiety or upset, then go to your fantasy of what innocence, simplicity, and Joy would look like.

Getting yourself into a physical space and setting that can enhance this state is always helpful. And if you have a spouse, lover, or deeply trusted friend who is willing to help you, ask him or her to be part of the process in whatever way you'd like, perhaps to tend to you lovingly, saying and doing those things which evoke the feeling of being nurtured, perhaps to hold you or stroke your forehead like a loving mother or father holding a baby. By all means, play some appropriate music. Engaging as many of the senses and memory-evoking stimuli as possible can only help to vivify the experience which is still alive within you.

Now, imagine the complete sense of safety and trust of childhood, the feeling of being utterly relaxed and at peace in the moment. There is no thought of having to do anything to feel safe and happy in the future, and no regret about anything of the past needing to be corrected. Spend some time getting in touch with this experience, immersing yourself as much as possible in innocent perception. You are free from fear, free from the need to defend against anything, and therefore free from the desire to think at all. You simply let yourself "be" instead, doing whatever your spontaneous Impulse suggests, whatever flows naturally from a sense of being taken care of by Life. If you have someone with you, let yourself ask for and receive whatever increases this feeling of being taken care of, facing any fear that would inhibit you from allowing this experience to come forth. Your attention floats wherever it would, discovering the delight of the senses, revealing all things in newness as you join in the dance of sensation and being.

Continue to allow your perception to awaken in this way, taking your practice into a moving meditation. Let the Impulse direct you to know the world by interacting with it. Everything calls to you as a great adventure, fascinating in its variety of shape and color, sound, feel, and taste. You look at the objects around you as if for the first time, mesmerized by the secrets they hold. You explore the mystery of sensation, breathing in deeply, letting the ground tickle your feet, the sunlight play through your closed eyelids. Run your hand under water, looking at the way the light jumps from the splash that comes off your hand, the sparkle of colors bursting forth from it.

Explore everything around you with a fresh perspective, getting down low on the ground or climbing up high to see the world in a new way. Discover your body as if you have never seen a body before, noticing its lines, textures, colors, patterns, and movements. Go outside and smell the flavors in the air, feel the breeze caress your cheek and smooth out your forehead. Or if it is cold, feel the tingle of the chill on the nape of your neck. Let the senses come alive for you, taking your mind out of its automatic rut, and practicing seeing and doing what is not usual for you. Let yourself settle deeply into the present, dropping down into the ground of Being, and see the miracle that is all around, here and now.

Look for and catch each limiting thought about what is possible, what life is about, how you should be spending your time and what you should be accomplishing. As you become aware of these thoughts, release the fear behind them and let yourself drop even more deeply into the present moment of simplicity. Allow the "thoughts" of Joy and Ease to emerge from behind these thoughts, creating a picture of an innocent world and a way of being that reflects that innocence. Without the jaded perception of a lifetime of limiting fears, we know infinite possibilities for delight in even the smallest of things. Our struggle to "become" somebody, a personality based on fear and defense, gives way to the experience of melting into the pleasure of being.

Now, ask yourself what is the "purpose" of life from this point of view? Of course, we didn't think in these terms as children. But we did have a sense of what was compelling, how we wanted to experience fulfillment, where our Impulse wanted to take us. Without the fearful thoughts, the urgencies, that impelled us to work frenetically toward a goal and "accomplish" ourselves, without the need to prove ourselves to others for some unnamed reward, we were free to "just be," to flow. We were free to fully become a part of, to lose ourselves in, the experience of being, joining with the whole of it in a close approximation of Oneness. Without the limits of our fears and defenses, who are you free to be? What are you free to do? How do you want to spend your time in the innocent experience of Joy? Write down your answers in your workbook, under the title *"What is the Purpose of Life from the Perspective of Innocence? What Do I Want to Do and Be?"*

## Exercise 2: Releasing Yourself for Vision

Next, using the "Flowchart for Your Life Journey" that you constructed in Chapter 3, we will see how the core fear and chief defense came up to take away this childlike Joy. We've felt lost to our innocence ever since, engaged in a sense of struggle, of "something's wrong and I must fix it." All our efforts throughout our life's journey have been devoted to trying to recover from this loss. Let us look now at the ways in which our fear and defense, while promising to help us return to Joy, have actually kept us from It. In so doing, we may release ourselves from these obstacles and discover the Vision waiting behind them.

For each of the life decisions in the flowchart, we will ask ourselves what would have happened if we had not made our choices out of fear, had not exercised defensiveness but allowed reality to be the way it was? Finding and facing the fears behind these decisions, bypassing the chief defense, is the key to finding our Vision. It brings us to the point of being completely willing for Vision to reveal itself. With no personal investment in a particular outcome and nothing to block our way, we are free to understand what Vision would have prescribed as our course of action, and what it prescribes still.

Using any of the exercises you have practiced so far, find and face the fears that caused you to make the choices you did. Imagine what it would have been like to do the opposite of what your chief defense caused you to do, and discover what choices you could have made instead. What choices would have met the needs of the situation more effectively? What choices would have served your life purpose? What choices would have allowed your basic drive for Joy to lead you? Write these down in your notebook under the heading, *"Without Fear and Defense, What Choices Would Have Served My Life Purpose?"*

Look for a pattern to emerge in your answers, a repeating theme that characterizes the message Joy has been wanting to express through you in each of these situations. Notice the way you have been consistently altering your course in life with a particular decision to protect yourself, to play it safe, to fulfill others' expectations, and so on. What is it that you have been wanting to do with your life instead? Who is it that you have been wanting to be? Write down the answer to these questions under the heading, *"What Have I Been Wanting to Do? Who Have I Been Wanting to Be?"*

Notice that in some way your answer is about getting back to the state you were in before the core fear first began. This time, however, it is with the difference of wanting to set things up so there is no possibility for the fear to return, for you or for others. Look for the pattern to emerge that will show you, in each of these situations, the primary drive behind all your decisions, how you would recreate the world of innocent Joy you once knew or imagined, and what the key ingredients would be to make this possible.

I once worked with someone who was driven to find perfection. In his spiritual life he wanted to experience full union with God, transcending the limitations and imperfections of the world. As he described this "vision," I understood that his quest was motivated by a fear of others' disapproval. In seeking a union with God, he hoped to escape from this fear.

Going through the process of releasing the fears and defenses of his life journey, he naturally discovered that in wanting to unite with God he was trying to re-create the union he knew with his mother in childhood. It was not that his desire to be with God was false. Rather, it was built on top of the deeper drive to recapture the experience he had as a child. If he wanted true union with God, he would have to release the defensiveness in his spiritual work, the attempt to force reality to look like his childhood. He would have to let go of the dependent relationship with his mother, and discover himself as an independent adult.

Through our therapy, he was able to fully individuate from his mother. As he did so, his spiritual work took on the flavor of an authentic Vision—he wanted to share himself with others, no longer re-creating a utopia for himself alone, safe from the fear of "outsiders." Expressing this freedom from fear, extending the Joy of his discovery of Self, he began conducting workshops in community building, finding the experience of union-with-God with other people.

## Exercise 3: The Picture of Fulfillment— Finding Your Vision

Now for finding our Vision. With the freedom from fear and the sense of where Joy has been wanting to take us, we will create the picture of fulfillment, the picture of our Joy fully expressed and realized. Again, this will be some form of your childhood vision of innocence, with the difference that comes with having lived the experience of fear and defense, transforming it, and harnessing its energy for a high Purpose.

Imagine that you are standing at the moment of your complete fulfillment. Everyone you love is around you, all fears and hurts from the past are resolved, and you are realizing your highest ideals for yourself and for the world. There is nothing incomplete about this picture; everything you have wanted is in place. The only need is to nurture and tend to this experience as it grows and expands in ever-widening circles.

Now ask yourself, "What would have to have happened in my life to bring me to this point? What would the specific steps and processes have been that would have led to this Vision of Joy? What are the components that carry its sense of ultimate Meaning and Purpose? And finally, what are the actions which translate these things into time and space?" Write the answers to these questions in your workbook, under the title *"Components of My Vision—The Picture of Fulfillment."*

As before, you will want to catch any limiting thoughts that keep you from the full-blown picture of fulfillment. Don't sell yourself short! This is your Vision and it will be the guiding principle of your life! Nothing less than radical Joy will satisfy you. Keep catching and releasing any limiting thoughts until you get to the answer that you know as the truth for you.

One hint for what to look for as you seek out your Vision: It will be big! It will stretch you to become far more than you knew you were, giving you the feeling of having "contributed your verse" to "the powerful play" of universal affairs. Without the littleness imposed by fear, your true stature will emerge and you will know your ability to move mountains if necessary, to realize your life's Purpose.

And be aware also of the fear that might say your Vision is not a "realistic possibility." You don't have to know yet how this Vision will be accomplished; all that is necessary is that you have the desire and commitment to do so. As we will see, the Vision may be as sweeping as "World peace" or as modest as "Healing all of my relationships." It may be as broad as "Feeding the hungry" or as focused as "Raising my child to be radically joyful." What will grow your Vision into something "soul-sized" will be the example you live for others, so that they, too, begin working for these goals. The Vision, at this point, grows *you* into its spokesperson, its caretaker, and you will find yourself being called upon to see it to full realization.

So let your spirit soar as you think about these things. Your spirit is far more expansive in its dreams, with the confidence to make good on them, than what fear would have you believe. You want to look for and cultivate an authentic sense of greatness as you consider these questions. This is not narcissistic;

the arrogance of narcissism is a fearful defense against inadequacy. In releasing fears we are not narcissistic, nor are we falsely humble; such humility is also a disguised attempt to "look good." It is not arrogance to presume to do great things, but simply the taking of your rightful place in the natural order of things.

As you write down your answers, keep asking yourself, "Is there anything more I can imagine wanting for myself or for the world beyond that?," expanding your Vision until you can declare yourself truly fulfilled, all your dreams realized, your Joy complete.

Remember, as you look for your Vision, it might be something from your core fear experience, because you are a master at that one. Life has prepared you perfectly as its ambassador for helping to relieve the suffering of others in your unique way. Sometimes the Vision is a matter of helping others bypass their chief defense and face their fears in the way you have learned to do. For you have an experience in this that no one else can match, having built all of your talents, skills, and "special gifts" in the process. You have used these talents to explore the ins and outs of what creates Joy, having found your unique answers in your unique ways. While these talents were born of defensiveness, exacting a cost and keeping you from relaxing into life, still they know the ways to Joy; they were designed for that. All that is needful is to release the fear that was driving them, to choose them with a free choice, if Joy says they are useful.

We may have all but given up on our talents and the dreams they were to help us achieve. The fear behind them inevitably wears us down to the point of exhaustion. This is when we live a life of obligation and burden, and try to settle for it. We may even have forgotten we had these dreams. Remember the possibilities of your childhood now, and resurrect your dreams! Call upon the talents you used to know, the things you used to excel at and which brought you Joy. Fear is out of the way and Vision is beckoning. And anything that can be used in its service is welcomed, invited, and encouraged.

If you are not receiving your Vision yet, if you cannot find what would fulfill you in this way, somewhere you are still invested in a particular outcome, not fully open to all possibilities. Go back and face the fear of having a Vision that you do not "like" or think you are suited for, and practice accepting it. With this, you may see such a possibility in a dramatically new light that opens up potentials in yourself you were not aware of.

You may also need to face the fear of never finding your Vision; fear can come in the form of being too eager, being afraid of failing in your Vision quest. This can be the very thing blocking your view of the Vision that is already being presented to you. The Vision *is* there; only we can block our awareness of it.

And consider as well the possibility that you have received your Vision but are discounting it with a defense that says, "I must understand it in a more literal way," or "I must be perfectly sure that I've understood it and understood it accurately." Find and release the fears behind these maneuvers, and the Vision you are receiving will prove its validity to you.

Finally, don't be concerned for now with how to live your Vision, how to take the appropriate actions and make it work in your life. At this point, we are developing our picture of a world transformed, free of the fear that has been distorting our view. In the next chapter, we will look at more specific ways the Vision wants to manifest itself in the various aspects of living. And, finally, we will integrate all this into a total package, the shape and structure of a fulfilling life, so that we may take the Vision into full-blown action!

# CHAPTER 8

# Ingredients for Whole Living

I went to the woods because I wanted to live deliberately.
I wanted to live deep and suck out all the marrow of
life. To put to rout all that was not life and not, when I
had come to die, discover that I had not lived.
—Henry David Thoreau, *Walden*

How does the Vision translate into the many areas of our lives
and become manifest in our very being? It must become our
new identity, casting off all that is not authentic in us, washing
away all tired and old habits that thwart the spontaneous
Impulse of Joy. It wants to express itself in ever-fresh and new,
creative and alive ways. It wants to consume the fears and
defenses that would hide the light in us, dissolving all darkness,
so that our Joy may shine unimpeded. And it wants to be lived
in each relationship, circumstance, and possibility we find
ourselves in. Let our every breath and thought be devoted to
what really matters. Let our every utterance speak of who we
truly are and what Reality is. Let our every action raise up the
ideals of what we most want to see happen for ourselves and
for the world.

In releasing fear, we call forth the Impulse-to-Joy, the expression of our true Self. Putting our Vision to work in every aspect of our lives is simply a matter of following this Impulse. But having lived with fear's restraints for so long, we may well be out of touch with what the Impulse is saying. We may despair that we are unable to hear its direction clearly, receiving only muffled and confused fragments, or perhaps nothing at all.

The most important key in tuning our receiver, now that our antennae are out, is to remember that the Impulse wants to express Life, and to express it abundantly! Under the reign of fear, we have come to live almost exclusively in our fear-based ideas about life, these ideas projecting outwardly as perception, imposed on top of the experience of reality-as-it-is. This results in a severely damped experience of the Impulse-to-Joy, a damping which would "hide our light under a bushel," keeping our Joy and enthusiasm tucked away in a dark corner. And this leads to depression and the loss of heart where Joy seems an impossibility.

We have been out of touch with our aliveness, perhaps for a long time. This is especially so in Western culture, where technology has made it so possible to be stagnant, divorced from the need to wrestle with survival issues and the exigencies of "real" life. But in this wrestling we contact our vital juices, the very experience of what it is to be in existence, the miracle of being alive. Like the butterfly fighting its way out of the cocoon, this meeting with the raw forces of life pumps blood through our veins, invigorating and enlivening us, so that we may feel Life coursing its way through us. We want to expose ourselves to the elements, fully confronting Existence in all its nakedness, so that we may know we are alive and experience the true meaning of Joy.

In the excessive pursuit of comfort, security, and predictability—the familiar trappings of defense—we believe we will find relief from our fear. Not only does this damp the Life Impulse, sedating our aliveness and burying our Joy, but it leaves the fear unresolved; our efforts are never enough to bring us real safety. We may fend off the fear for a time but are always aware that our defenses can break down, the fear rushing in to overwhelm us.

We must become more interested in Freedom and Joy than in security. For what is the use of our security if we have no Joy? Is it not better to have Joy and no security than to have all the security in the world but no Joy? As we become free from the fear of not having security, we naturally move toward where there is the greatest amount of Life happening, the greatest expression of Love, the greatest flow of Energy.

Life is attracted to Life. Being fully alive means seeing the futility of our old ways, the ways of strain, boredom, and life-lessness. It means giving up our love affair with the fears that supply these habits and "stepping back" from them. It means simply watching their seduction as they attempt to lure us into response. It means celebrating as they dissolve into a mirage when we fail to jump into the picture and energize it with our thoughts. And then it means being free! Expressing the Life Impulse, following its lead. We no longer make our decisions of how to live according to what we personally want or what is safe—the prescriptions of fear. It doesn't matter what we do, as long as we are expressing Life most abundantly and increasing our Joy and the Joy of others as we do so.

Our next task involves looking at each of the ingredients for whole living and discerning the fears and limitations that have held us back from fulfillment in these areas. With this awareness, we release the fear and ask ourselves, "What is possible for me now? Where does my Impulse move me now that I have given up fear?" This provides the necessary foundation for living our Vision, the fertile soil in which to plant and grow our ideals. It is the "getting our house in order" that makes living our Vision possible.

Here, then, are the "Ingredients for Whole Living," in which the Life Impulse wants to express itself through us:

- "Meaningful work"
- "Relationships that work" (including "Fully expressed sexual relating")
- "Community—Reclaiming our tribes"
- "Mastering health" (including "Physical exercise for priming the Life Impulse")
- "Contact with the rhythms of nature"
- "Creative expression"
- "Adventures in consciousness"

These ingredients may need to be tailored to your particular circumstances. But remember, circumstances do not have the power to limit Joy. It is still and always a matter of releasing the fears that come up along the way. So, for example, if you have a physical incapacity, your practice in the "Mastering health" section may be about working with any fear or upset you might have around this condition. Such a practice creates physical flow, as the life force is freed from resistance. Similarly, if you are practicing communication with someone who is unwilling to join you in the practice, know that it is necessary only for you to clear out the fears that were obstructing *your* expression. If the other does not receive the communication, you have a perfect opportunity to practice releasing any upset or fear that may arise in response.

The exercises in this chapter are to be done continuously, first to get your life into the shape you want it, then to maintain it there. This is a "lifestyle fitness program," incorporating the basic ingredients for healthy, whole living. These are the tools for bringing our Vision into the everyday world. In the following chapter, we will work with the structures for organizing these tools into a lifestyle. Do not be concerned yet with how to put it all together in a comprehensive program. As we will see, it is the Vision which will direct and inform such a task.

# EXERCISES

The exercises in this chapter are simply a matter of freeing ourselves from the fears that have kept us from fulfillment, the full expression of who we are, in each of the areas of whole living. Essentially, this is a matter of performing a Vision quest specifically around each such area, first laying out the itinerary we want to travel and then removing any roadblocks of fear that come along the way.

## Exercise 1: Meaningful Work

In looking for the fears that would keep us from finding meaningful work, there are two main categories to consider: We may be caught (1) by the fear of changing our work circumstances, or (2) by the fear of doing what it takes to make our present work meaningful.

To determine which of these two is primary in us and which fear should therefore be faced, we follow the first of the "Rules for Making Choices" in Chapter 6. That is, we practice becoming completely willing to face the fear of changing our work situation and completely willing to face the fear of not doing so.

If this reveals that we are to make our present work situation meaningful, then we recognize that every moment represents an opportunity for choosing fear or Joy. Just as in the Vision quest, we do not want to assume that our environment needs to be changed. This runs the risk of having us think that fulfillment comes from outside, that it is not solely determined by the thoughts we choose to think and the perception we choose to manifest.

In *Way of the Peaceful Warrior*, the main character meets a master who, of all things, is pumping gas at a gas station. This is both his means for earning income as well as the optimal lifestyle for his Vision. Each time customers come up to the pump, they get a teaching, specially tailored to their needs, as well as gasoline. It is not our job or its particular circumstance that creates the opportunity for making our work meaningful. It is the way we are relating to our job and circumstances—through fear or Joy—that determines their meaning and value.

So meaningful work, if you are not to make a change in circumstances, is a matter of finding and facing the fears that are keeping you from Joy in your present job. Joy must mean, however, that you are fulfilling your life purpose, your Vision, in everything you do. Therefore, ask yourself these questions:

- Is my present work promoting the values that I subscribe to, promoting the cause of Oneness and Joy, rather than separation and fear?
- Are my relationships at work expressions of the Joy I want to manifest?
- Where, if others are meeting me with attack, can I respond to their "call for Love" with fearlessness and the example of "a better way"?
- Where at work am I on "autopilot," operating from routine, security, and the fulfilling of expectation, rather than listening to the prescription of Joy in a fresh way each moment?

If, in facing the fears of both staying in or leaving your present job, you find that you are to change employment, then you want to take the necessary actions for creating a new career, one that is congruent with your Vision. Some of the primary fears that may come up with this are the fear of not making enough money; not having enough free time; working too hard or having too much responsibility; or not having the opportunity to realize your Vision. Once you have worked through these fears, as they may apply, then you may begin designing your optimal work, asking the question: How do I want my work to promote my Vision, in its particular details and its general effect on the world?

Let us look more closely at these fears. The first is about security. Fear would have us make more money or accumulate more possessions than needed. It would require us to sacrifice more time and compromise our purpose, as security becomes the end rather than the means. Money and possessions are neutral; they can be used in the service of what is highest and finest in us, or they can become the hook upon which we hang our fears. Working through such fears, we may become free of the need to accumulate more than what serves our Vision. If we are to change our work life, let it be for the fulfillment of Joy, rather than another testament to security. Our goal is to fully live, not merely survive.

The question of time is equally amenable to our free choice. Too often, we live to make money rather than make money to live. And with this comes a vicious cycle wherein we must protect the money we have made. This protection requires that we make more money, which then must be better protected, and so on. This is the greater part of what eats up our time! Without the need to accumulate, there is a freedom and flexibility to design our use of time in the ways that are most appropriate for the fulfillment of our Vision.

As we progress in our practice, we will spontaneously and courageously find creative ways to make more time. Consider, for example, the fear of asking others for help. Our Vision, if we are listening truly, is going to be too large for us to accomplish in isolation. Facing the fear of asking others for help, we will find ways to interface with them as they live their Visions, delegating and coordinating tasks that multiply our efforts and maximize our time.

As for the fear of working too hard, taking on too much responsibility, we want to realize that there is nothing we would rather be working for, or spending our time on, than our Vision. And so it cannot be considered a burden or heavy responsibility. Whatever the requirement, whether it be the need to make a certain amount of money to realize your Vision, to complete further schooling or training to make your new career possible, or to give up comfort or status so that you may be free to do what is important to you, understand that it is your Joy to do so. Responsibility and hard work may be reinterpreted as the challenge of living life fully. Instead of burden and fatigue, we become invigorated by Purpose and the promise of Fulfillment.

But again, be aware of the fear that would have you giving up security or taking on too much work too quickly or irresponsibly. Joy can only come if we are being "responsible" in the sense of recognizing what is needed to have things work effectively. To give up security too quickly, or to take on too many obligations when we have not sufficiently worked through our fear, may give an appearance of freedom. But the fear will surely come up if we have not dislodged it from its home in us, to rob us of this freedom and create unjoyful consequences.

If you fear that there will not be the opportunity to realize the work of your Vision, then know this: What you love to do is what others love as well. Do not be afraid of the idea that too many people are doing it or it is not worthy of being paid for. Become intimately familiar with it and see what is needed to have it live and thrive in the world. Then pour yourself into it and persevere. Your Joy will naturally have you looking for the opportunities to fulfill itself, and in the expression of your passion, others will know you as the one who represents this work. In this way, you will find your opportunity and your audience.

We are here to learn the unique lessons that only being in a body can provide. And this requires feeding, housing, watering, and clothing the body. But without fear, this is not the problem or the time consumer we imagine it to be. Our work should be an expression of our Love and not our fear. We have devoted ourselves too much to the garnering of security, the protecting and adorning of the body. These things are a poor substitute for the Joy we seek. They are not wrong in and of themselves, but their only value comes in whether they increase our Joy. All too often they but distract us temporarily from our fear and insecurity.

Releasing the fear that motivates such efforts reveals that, indeed, our needs are very few, while the opportunities for doing our right work are many. When it is necessary to "compromise" on our Joy so that we may take care of the body or build for future goals, let us practice the understanding that, without fear, these things become the stepping-stones toward our Purpose. Keeping our sights set on our Vision, our *choice* to take care of practicalities becomes a further expression of that which make Joy possible.

So face your fears and do what fills you with Joy. For once we have begun releasing fear, we experience a Joy that naturally wants to extend toward others. And this is what our life's Work should be. Let our work be nothing but this extension of Joy, this Freedom, no fear driving us that says we have to work to please others, to avoid rejection, or to meet imagined security needs. These are all really fear in disguise. None of them helps us meet our needs or fulfill our Vision.

Of course we must take care of the basics for survival—this is part of what it takes to live our Vision successfully. But without fear, such efforts become the opportunity to express our Joy, and our every moment becomes the meaningful work that builds toward the fulfillment of our ideals.

## Exercise 2: Relationships That Work

Relationships are absolutely central in the path to Joy. But our relationships are also the cause of some of our greatest suffering. Too often, we feel woefully inadequate when it comes to making our relationships "work."

Of course, it is fear that sits at the source of trouble. Fear would have us believe that we depend upon others to make us whole, complete, and happy. They become the objects of our need, the imagined source of our fulfillment. This confirms the illusion that we are not whole within. We, therefore, become afraid of the possibility that they will not do their part in our fantasy. We twist and distort ourselves in incredible ways to secure their love, insisting that reality bend to our wishes, that others confirm our illusions about ourselves. Knowing we do not truly have such control, we fear for our success, imagining we will be left incomplete, bereft, and always wanting.

There are two primary ways this fear manifests in relationships. One is the fear of being with people when they fail to comply with our wishes. The other is the fear of not being with them at all. We cycle between these two, sometimes seeking aloneness so that no one will "bother" us, and sometimes seeking companionship, but having to control its circumstances to minimize the threat of abandonment or deprivation. In short, we are afraid of being with others and afraid not to be; we want to be alone but are terrified of isolation.

The desire to be alone is usually the fear of "dealing" with others. Unless we have come to peace with our relationships and have worked through this fear, the desire to be alone is escapism. Sometimes this is a necessary protection to establish our sense of boundaries. Otherwise, it is the experience of separation that keeps us from finding our Joy.

On the other hand, our fear of being alone often has us clinging to others, taking care of them, fulfilling their expectations of us and sacrificing ourselves in the process. These are the defenses against abandonment. We may be run by the idea that we need the approval of others or that we must protect them from their fears in order to feel safe ourselves. All such ideas are built on the faulty assumption that we are not already safe and something threatens our integrity, our wholeness. And this assumption is itself built on the dream of a separated self.

Our task, then, is to discover the freedom to be with others without the need to defend. For it is this need that has us wanting to escape from or wanting to cling to others. We must release the fear that being in relationships will deprive us of what we think we need as well as the fear that we must sacrifice ourselves to avoid abandonment.

Without these fears, we no longer project our emptiness in such a way that we see the integrity of who we are as dependent upon others. Once free of the fearful need to control others, we will not subtly attack them, manipulate them, or make them feel guilty if they do not do our bidding. And they will not need to do the same in return. Our relationships become the opportunity to express our sense of wholeness and completion, a statement of the Oneness we feel within extended out to join with others.

So living your Vision with respect to relationships means facing the fear of being alone and facing the fear of being with others. To face the fear of being alone, take some time, in actuality or in imagination, exploring the experience of what it would be like to be abandoned by all—forever! Don't worry, it's just a fear-thought. If you do the "What happens next?" exercise, for example, you will find that settling into the experience of aloneness leads to a dissolution of your individual sense of self and a joining with the All.

To face the fear of being with others, find all the ways you avoid being fully yourself with them and do the opposite of what your fear tells you to do. As in the exercise on sharing private thoughts, full communication becomes one of your primary tools here. Also look for the fear behind your unjoyous responses to others, and let go of the judgments, assigned meanings, and interpretations you make upon them, using whichever of the exercises you prefer.

## Fully Expressed Sexual Relating

These same principles apply in our sexual relationships—in Technicolor! Intimacy is the experience of having no barriers or separation, rediscovering our Oneness with others. Being fully intimate does not mean only sexual intimacy, but sex can be a potent tool for breaking down barriers. Alternatively, it can be a great reinforcer for our illusions of need, fostering feelings of emptiness and the dependency on others to fill us up. When used in the service of Oneness, however, sex can be a powerful way to discover our true Self. It is the physical name of Love, the sensual face of Joy.

But even sex can become stale, giving little of the true experience of being fully alive. When defenses have us locked up inside, unable to relax our walls to join with our partner, we fall into a routine of "going through the motions." The key to "great sex," holy sex, is in releasing such defenses, letting the Life Impulse flow through us without obstacle, fully expressing ourselves without fear. We reveal our "private thoughts" by sharing in a physical way the fullness of who we are.

Sex is, indeed, communication, a wonderful vehicle for soul contact. It can be a beautiful experience of Oneness, breaking down the separating barriers of "self-ness," and fostering a mutual caring where another's needs become as important as our own. No longer trying to "get" from the other, to have them fill our emptiness, the boundaries melt and we have a close approximation of what it is to be One.

But with this power, sex also has the potential for bringing up so much of that which we have defended against, revealing those things we have tried to keep hidden about ourselves, confronting us with our powerlessness to control the other and make our fantasies come true. We would hide all that we think would cause us to be rejected, presenting a mask of "perfection." In this way, we hope to please the other, who is caught in their own fantasy that we will fill their emptiness. We try to control so that the other will love us perfectly, falling heavily into the delusion that our Joy depends on something outside ourselves. And by our command they must likewise fulfill our fantasy perfectly, providing the opportunity for us to come out from hiding, promising never to reject us for that which we are daring to reveal about ourselves, our deepest desires, longings, and wants.

In the best of relationships, until the fear is worked through, we feel the tremendous insecurity that all this will fall apart. And so we anxiously check out the other's every minutest response, verifying whether they will fulfill our fantasy. In the worst of relationships, we know the devastation of heartbreak, the direct experience of our fear come true, the ripping away from Oneness and the sentencing to an eternity of isolation.

And yet, we push forth to Joy, and sex, intimacy, and relationship are ever the guides and teachers on our path. We cannot be satisfied with fear's answer to remain in perpetual solitude. Touching, expressing our true Self, revealing private thoughts, sharing the impulse to connect—these are the means by which communication becomes communion, and our relationships take us "Home" to Joy.

## Exercise 3: Community—Reclaiming Our Tribes

We live in relationship to everything. Extending our sphere of Oneness, we recognize the need for community. For we cannot accomplish our Vision in isolation; it must live in the larger matrix of community. The very nature of Vision is that which works toward the realization of Oneness. Our attempt to find Joy in isolation is one of the great crippling forces of our society. When Mother Teresa came to America for the first time, she remarked that the isolation and loneliness she saw in this land of so much physical wealth was some of the greatest poverty she had ever seen.

Again, we cannot do it alone. Community gives the support for working through our fears that makes it all possible in the first place. When St. Francis's father would meet him on the streets of Assisi, he would curse and scorn him in a most abusive way. Francis, with a commitment to transforming his personal hurt into love for others, learned to ask his brothers to whisper words of support at such times, reminders about who he really was and what he was committed to.

This is community. It is a primary ingredient for expressing the Life Impulse and being fully alive. The epidemic of isolation and loneliness comes from the separating forces of fear. We believe we want our "freedom" and our "independence." These are important goals, but when twisted by fear they can become a prison cell, locking us in away from others and away from Joy. Our goal must be freedom *in* our relationships, and independence from the need to control or be controlled by others.

The "sangha," or community, is one of Buddhism's "three treasures," something to "take refuge in." Community is the laboratory within which we cultivate our Vision. In our community, our tribe of kindred spirits, there is an agreement, perhaps unspoken, to support each other on the path, and a deep trust in the caring and commitment that come with this. There are still fears to be worked through, just as with all relationships. But there is also an implicit certainty that no misunderstanding will cause an ultimate breach in your support for and caring of each other. This gives the safety that makes it possible to face our fears in the other areas of our lives, as we work toward the fulfillment of our Vision.

Start with those you already feel comfortable and safe with. If there is no one with whom you feel this level of safety, then by all means go out to create it. You may have to face your fears of initiating contact, but remember, everyone wants and in fact needs what you are offering.

Once you have gathered your initial group, ask them to join you in a conscious intention of creating community together. One ready "excuse" is to invite them to go through the practices of this book with you and begin a study group for "Radical Joy." Tell them you want to build a trust that no matter what truth you reveal to each other, you will feel an implicit acceptance. Tell them that with this trust you want their support in learning to accept others, in facing all the fears that come up along the way toward this goal. Then put it into practice, sharing private thoughts, letting go of meanings and judgments, doing the opposite of what defense says to do. Deepen your relationship with them, risking rejection, trusting in your safety.

Next, take the strength you are developing in your community out into the world. As you build your strength this way, releasing fears and cultivating full intimacy, you extend your practice to include other relationships, so that they, too, may become part of your community in an ever-expanding sphere.

In our highest Vision, our community will be the whole world. No fears will block our intimacy with anyone. It is said that the test of whether you are practicing peace is if anyone who comes in contact with you shares in your peace. Until that time, we work toward this state, extending our circle of Joy by releasing any fears that come up with each person we meet.

## Exercise 4: Mastering Health (Including Physical Exercise for Priming the Life Impulse)

Health is the natural result of releasing fears. Our bodies reflect tensions in very exact ways even though the pattern may not be immediately apparent. Finding and facing our fears, including the fear of pain and sickness, is the key to mastering health.

Physical exercise, stretching, and other methods that pump energy through the body become important tools for developing and maintaining vitality. You may want to begin a practice of Tai Chi, yoga, or anything else that will break up the blockages of fear imposed on the body. All these are really a matter of allowing our natural health, the expression of our Joy, to flow freely through us.

Fear can make it too easy, seductive even, to let the body stagnate. For this reason, it is essential to engage in a regular practice of some form of exercise, getting the juices really flowing. Only fear has us seek the "comfort" of sedating ourselves with television and junk food. Freedom from fear moves us to invigorate the body, breathing fully and priming the vital juices of life energy. It is exhilarating, invigorating . . . it tells you that you are alive! Find and face whatever fear-thoughts run through your mind to convince you not to engage in such a program. And draw upon your community (workout partners?) for support.

## Exercise 5: Contact with the Rhythms of Nature

Contact with Nature is contact with our natural selves. It is restoring and awakening our internal rhythms as they come into sync with those of Nature. We have grown so alienated from the natural environment—"reality-as-it-is." How can we possibly know ourselves and be fully alive when living in four walls, breathing in forced air, and never feeling the refreshing cold of winter or the loving embrace of a warm summer sun, never focusing on the miniature world of a tiny insect, never watching a sunrise or a sunset?

We want to allow the Life Impulse to express itself through our bodies, interacting with the Life Impulse as it is being expressed through the Body of Nature. Aliveness in this way means engaging the senses fully in the splendor and fascination of Nature's pageantry. It means dancing, singing, jumping, climbing, breathing deeply, adventuring, swimming, running freely. Once again, our prescription for whole living involves doing the opposite of what fear would have us do, using our bodies as do children, who know no defensiveness or tension, expressing our Joy without restraint.

But we have many fears to face in order to restore our natural selves. We have a fear of getting dirty, of being wild and "uncivilized," of finding ourselves without all the necessities of life planned and secured, of being exposed to cold and hunger. In our genetic memory, we still hold the fear of being eaten by other animals. We fear the feeling of being infinitesimally small in the face of Nature's vastness. Ultimately, we fear disappearing into the void of nothingness, as we confront our individual unimportance in an impersonal universe.

All these fears must be faced, slowly, steadily, courageously. We must stop devoting ourselves so mercilessly to the religion of security and social "appropriateness," and follow the Life Impulse as it moves with the rhythms of our natural selves. Spending time in Nature, listening to the rhythms of the body and following its impulse, watching the animals and the cycles of death and rebirth, will show us what fears need to be faced and when. But we must reconnect with our wildness if we are to be whole, if we are to be fully alive.

When we begin to heal from these fears, we begin also to feel a great power welling up within us. With our feet planted deeply into the earth, we begin drawing up, like a tree soaking up groundwater, the power of the mighty earth. This *is* the experience of the Life Impulse! When we access this huge source of energy, our own energy field naturally expands and seeks to join with the whole of Nature. In the "Don Juan" books of Carlos Castaneda, one of the shamans literally begins swimming in the earth, for it is the only way he can "hug" the whole thing at once!

We feel our aliveness with the earth and we want to merge with it by dancing, singing, drumming, and chanting. We want to make love and swing from trees, to stand in a fierce wind, soaking up all its power and then roaring it back out. Once this experience of power is fully resolved so that we have embraced the whole, we no longer need to push against limits.

We realize that nothing can threaten us, we are one with it all, we *are* the all of it and it is us. With this, we become naturally gentle, quiet, and our chant of power turns into a lullaby, a sweet song, a caress.

Some of the most magical days of my life were spent deep in the woods taking a wilderness program in the Pine Barrens of New Jersey. Living very much as a "tribe" in the Native American tradition, we were completely cut off from the influences of modern society. No clocks, no artificial environments—just a flow with the daily rhythms of Nature. A peace settled upon us during those days which was like nothing I've felt since childhood. Whatever represented the need of the moment, as told by the whispering of the winds and the movement of the grasses, that was where our Impulse took us. Meaningful work took the form of basic interactions with Nature and with meeting our needs—gathering wild edibles, crafting tools for building shelter. A natural sense of community and harmony developed between us as we lost the need for self-protection and our true selves emerged. Life became a series of unfolding moments whose purpose was fulfilled in the discovery and sharing of Joy together.

## Exercise 6: Creative Expression

In our search for whole living we need a flow of fresh perspective, a fullness in our contact with creation, adventure, and wonder. We need to play and dance as the expression of our aliveness in this world of form. And we need to make our contribution by creating new forms. But for this to be possible, we must break out of the ordinary, daring to be a little outrageous, to venture out of comfort zones. We must face our fear and try new things, rather than staying safe and limited in a routinized existence. We must dare to defy expectation. These are the colors of creativity!

To expand creative expression, become aware of how fear

leads you to make choices and accomplish tasks out of habit. Then, with the principle of doing the opposite of what fear says to do, find new ways to experience or act on these tasks, or reinvent them altogether. Play with the sensations of your back against the seat you are sitting in, the feel of this book on your skin, the texture of your socks on your feet.

Purposefully get off the beaten track, change your schedule, take a walk in the middle of the night, or call someone for no particular reason. Take a drive somewhere or put yourself in a situation where life is happening and then break out of the mold of ordinariness, trying new things, creating adventure, facing fears, going right up to someone and initiating a connection. Use the body, move, dance, exercise, to fall into Flow. Consider the possibility of bringing a particular form of creative expression—perhaps composing music, choreographing dance, painting, or writing poetry—into your daily life, but as always, be willing to change such a plan at a moment's notice. For such spontaneity is the true creative expression, where life becomes your art form and each moment a new stroke of the brush.

## Exercise 7: Adventures in Consciousness

Reality is certainly a larger affair than what our assigned meanings, based on the limitations of fear, would have us believe. Without fear, we communicate with higher orders of reality, communing with or becoming one with more and more of the totality of things. Potentials we didn't know were possible open up as we literally identify with other aspects of reality, seeing through the eyes of new perspective. Each such opening brings us closer to the Grand Perspective, wherein we see everything as one, knowing it all as it knows itself.

There is a need for the Life Impulse to express itself in our personal expansion, our spiritual evolution, as we explore this thing called consciousness and help it grow. Traditional cultures from around the world have developed their own tools, including the shamanic journey, using the sonic drive of repetitive drumming, chanting in chords (literally singing more than one note at the same time), altered breathing techniques, and sensory deprivation. One group of monks undergoes an initiatory training requiring them to live in a cave in total darkness for an extended period of time. To pass the initiation, they must find a way to illuminate the cave from within themselves!

First, spend some time exploring the question: What is it to be conscious? How does sensory information register on our awareness? How is it possible to have thoughts? What is the nature of the hum "inside" our heads that tells us we are alive, that we are aware, that we have been turned "on"? Look at these questions with a fresh perspective, getting in touch with what it is to have this most miraculous gift called consciousness.

Next, begin exploring ways to change your state of consciousness, to shift your experience of reality so that what seemed dull and lifeless now becomes intense and electrifying! Find ways of focusing your consciousness into a singular groove. Let it create a trancelike state with your attention completely immersed in a single point. The busy-ness of your mind's usual chatter becomes silent, time stops, and your awareness of being located in a specific point in space disappears. Continue playing with the infinite variety of states of consciousness, identifying first with the observing self and then directing the ways in which you use your attention. Follow the lead of your Impulse-to-Joy, letting it open you to a sense of mystery and adventure.

## Exercise 8: Recipe for Our Lives—"Training Camp"

When we are living our Vision, stopping for no fear that would block the full and spontaneous expression of who we are, then Joy naturally expresses itself as that which brings all things into right order, flow, harmony. This becomes our moment-to-moment prescription for living, where we are in action, guided by pure ideals, doing what we are moved to do and not what fear and obligation would insist we do. The Impulse-to-Joy expresses itself through us, as we "sing the music within," letting nothing stand in the way to mute our song.

Some might take the freedom from fear to be a license for irresponsibility and decadence. This does not promote Joy; it does not make for a life that works. For fear still rules, albeit in secrecy, in that the true Impulse is not free to take on the responsibility for making things work.

There is certainly a responsibility that comes with freedom. Indeed, we become responsible for everything we encounter or even think about, realizing that its shape and character depend on the perceptions we choose to have about it, the meanings we choose to assign to it. Make no mistake; this has "real" effects on our lives and on the lives of those in our world. We must take this responsibility very seriously. Life wants to be lived, and lived fully, and it is our charge to see to it that this Vision is fulfilled. We cannot do so without accepting our responsibility for infusing all things with Joy by our chosen perceptions.

But this does not mean we are to consider the responsibility in a fearful way. For with the responsibility that comes with freedom comes the freedom to be responsible. It is not we, as separate selves, who choose how to act responsibly, but rather the Impulse-to-Joy, the one Self within all of us, which chooses and finds no resistance in us.

Take a day or half a day, or a weekend or more if possible, for a "sabbatical" from fear. During this time, commit yourself to following the pure Impulse for Joy, choosing moment-to-moment to release fear and listen to Joy's promptings. For this period of time, let fear make no decisions about how you will act, but let the Impulse move you wherever it would, revealing the secret of radical Joy, of being fully alive.

In the experience of whole living, we do not need to plan defensively for how to get our needs met. Rather, we simply listen for Joy's Impulse in each moment. For now, while we are building up our capacity for this, we make the preparations and arrange the circumstances as we can, to create the opportunity to practice choosing without fear.

For the early stages, then, set aside the time and resources you may need, and clear your schedule of obligations in advance. Remove those things from your environment which would tempt you into old patterns, and set up other things which will support your success. You may want to take the phone off the hook, unplug the television, or bring along some favorite music. You may even want to bring along some favorite people, but make sure they are in full agreement with the sole purpose of the project, so the experience does not regress into habitual modes of fear and routine. Prepare in whatever way is helpful to you. Again, until we are completely willing to make any radical changes in our lives that Joy would suggest, we want to simulate the conditions of such freedom as much as possible for this project, even if it is somewhat artificial or contrived at first.

Once you have arrived in this "training camp," follow the rules for making choices, using all the various tools presented in the book to release fear, so that you may be available to hear Joy's direction. If, as you begin your practice, you are having difficulty hearing this direction, then there is still some fear at work to be sought out and faced.

To jump-start past this block, imagine doing something you know is fun, Joyful, or fulfilling. The feeling of fun, joy, or fulfillment as you imagine doing this thing *is* the Impulse-to-Joy. Then, see what fears come up to prevent you from acting on that Impulse. These are the same fears blocking you from hearing Joy's direction and knowing what to do *right now*. Remember, if there seems to be some "real" limit imposed upon you by circumstance, such as a physical incapacity or a lack of money, then know that beyond the *form* of what you were moved to do is the *content* of Joy waiting to be expressed in a different way. Let go the attachment to the form and let the Impulse move you. Be prepared for the possibility of a "healing" of that which you thought limited you, as you release the fear in this way.

In your practice, look for the shifts in perception that tell you of the true nature of whole living, of what life is meant to be like here. The "limits" of being in a body and having to serve its needs, urges, and desires, even the "limits" of space and time, are not true limits. Without fear, our experience of these things becomes a further testimony to Joy, describing the shape of it, creating the arenas in which it wants to be lived, in this particular description of existence called human beingness. Without fear, our body and its needs become a beautiful expression of the flow of the Life Force in a way which we can feel. Without fear, time and space become the great freedoms, sacred playgrounds in which we dance out our Joy, writing the poems of our lives as Joy would have us do.

# CHAPTER 9

# RADICAL JOY: THE VISION FULFILLED

If a man is called to be a streetsweeper, he should sweep the streets as Michelangelo painted, or Beethoven composed music, or Shakespeare wrote poetry. He should sweep streets so well that all the hosts of heaven and earth will pause and say, here lived a great streetsweeper who did his job well.

—Martin Luther King, Jr.

Gandhi's life was a magnificent example of the commitment to Vision. He wanted to see India emancipated from England, and he wanted it to happen nonviolently. He gave himself completely to this end.

From the first moment of his calling, where standing on principle, he submitted to the beatings of the British police, he surrendered all personal agendas. Willing to change his approach at any instant, he followed the direction of things instead of imposing his plans upon the situation. Through unendingly creative means, he put the practice of high commitment into action. People started gathering around the force of his conviction.

Continually transferring his perception from "meeting attack with attack" to a nonviolent stand with the Truth that was immune to such attack, Gandhi rendered England powerless. Eventually, the strength of his nonviolent resistance caused England to loosen its grip where no amount of forceful resistance could. India would be free.

The next "enemy," the fear of his own people, would be harder to subdue. A civil war broke out over Hindu versus Muslim rights in the newly independent India. Only the purest expression of Truth and Vision could overwhelm the power of personal wills and defenses against fear. Time and again, violence broke out as the forces of fear-turned-into-anger erupted. But Gandhi provided such expression of Truth by living his Vision as if he had no choice.

One of his means for doing this was the fast. At first he would fast in protest. A long, painful fast that forced people's attention away from fighting and on to him. Eventually, when the fighting would break out again, Gandhi had become so fused with his Vision that, if the Vision could not live, he could not live. He literally gave up the will to preserve his life as long as the violence continued. Whole populations now were fighting, as the power of the energies he unleased for Good turned dark through the agency of fear. Gandhi declared he would not break his fast until the fighting stopped completely. This was, it seemed, a death sentence.

Such a proclamation shocked the people into awareness of what their fears had wrought. They could no longer deny reality-as-it-was. Their love for Gandhi, for the ideal he represented of a peaceful world, forced them to face their fears. They knew that if they continued fighting, the ideal would die. Their fear would have caused its death.

The fighting did begin to stop. People begged Gandhi to end his fast and nourish himself back to health. But he refused until they could prove to him that the fighting had stopped completely and that it would not start again.

As word of this went out, enemies, now joined in a common purpose and Vision, found ways to end their fighting and came together in a demonstration of harmony. The day

Gandhi broke his fast, not one outbreak of violence had been reported. A new cooperation was being born.

The final piece in our tapestry of Joy is to weave in a mechanism by which the Vision takes root and grows, extends and spreads until it reaches out beyond ourselves. We want others to "catch" our Vision, so that what is in our head becomes a Vision rooted solidly in everyday reality. When others catch the Vision we have spoken, it locks us into our commitment. People begin looking to us as a voice for the Vision. And in this, we acquire a new identity; we become the pure expression of the Vision, the vehicle through which it lives.

The key to this is to make commitments to others in a way that forces us to put our Vision into action. Having made such commitments, we have a powerful antidote to the seductions of fear which would draw us away from our commitment; others are now involved and have started counting on us to fulfill our promises, the forces of intention being put into motion. This is not dependency but interdependency, an expression of our true interconnectedness. As the Chinese proverb says, "When you sneeze, it wiggles the sun!" We want to lock ourselves into this kind of relationship with the world, teaching the Vision of our highest ideals. When everyone is living their Vision and making their commitments to each other, the world returns to harmony and perfect working order.

We must put the Vision into action where it is having effects on others, so that these others start taking actions that force us to continue with our part. Ultimately, our Vision takes on a life of its own; even if we were to try to back out of it, or if we were somehow unable to continue with it, it gets carried forward by the momentum of the movement we have begun.

Gandhi, again, gives us inspiration in this. One evening, as he prepared to give a lecture on the right to be self-governing, British officers notified in advance of his "seditious" lecture came to arrest him, attempting to thwart his efforts and cancel the presentation. Immediately his wife began to follow him as he was being escorted to jail. One of the officers said to her, "You don't have to come, Mrs. Gandhi, just your husband." To this, she replied, "If you take my husband, I will speak in his place tonight and you will then have to arrest me too." As they began carting her off as well, a third person came forth to be arrested, declaring they were next in line to speak for the lecture, and on and on it went. Realizing there were too many people to be jailed, the British officers were powerless to carry out their duty and the lecture went on as scheduled. The impact of the news of this was such that what began as an attempt to thwart Gandhi's efforts gave tremendous impetus to the movement.

It is essential, then, that the Vision grow beyond what we personally can carry. We must not leave our "soulwork" as nothing more than a pretty sentiment and lifeless ideal. We must breathe life into it, like fanning a new flame, until it sparks into something befitting the fire of our spirit. And then, if we would see the world transformed by our Vision, we must share it with others. Joy is no longer a matter of attaining personal goals. It springs from the desire to serve the higher Good. Only in this can we find the true Fulfillment we seek. The natural extension of our Joy is to share it and help others be transformed by it, so that it may grow, multiply, and raise the world.

## EXERCISES

In these exercises, we will grow the roots of our Vision, creating structures that anchor us solidly into seeing it through to fruition. When fear's distractions try to derail us, these structures force us to walk straight through the fear toward our goal. With this, we become unstoppable.

It is especially critical at this point to remember that circumstance does not have the power, at all, to limit us in living fully. The by-now famous quote attributed to Goethe reminds us that when we release our fears, the veil is drawn from our eyes. At once we see the limitless opportunities for fulfillment that were invisible to us when fear's blinders had us focus only on how to stay safe:

> Until you are committed, there is hesitancy, the chance to draw back, always ineffectiveness, concerning all acts of initiative (and creation). There is one elementary truth, the ignorance of which kills countless ideas and splendid plans: The moment you definitely commit yourself, then Providence moves, too. All sorts of things occur to help you that would never otherwise have occurred. A whole stream of events issues from the decision, raising in your favor all manner of unforeseen incidents and meetings and material assistance, which no one could have dreamed would have come your way. Whatever you can do, or dream you can, begin it. Boldness has genius, power and magic in it.

When we set the goal first, without consideration for fear or circumstance, we know our direction clearly enough that when circumstance tries to push us off course, it merely becomes the opportunity to redirect ourselves toward the goal.

Of course, that which would keep us from taking our commitments seriously, or even making them in the first place, is fear. Again, we will look at the core fear that has tried to convince us that we can get away without making or keeping such commitments, that the risk of failure is too great or that it is too much responsibility having others depend on us for their Visions. At the same time, we must be wise to the subtler fear that would cause us to take our commitments too seriously, where we feel bound to them out of the fear of disappointing others, not pleasing God, or fulfilling our higher destiny. Remember, this is only about Joy, not guilt or obligation, and we want to include ourselves among those the Vision serves.

Certainly, we must yield our personal wishes and "compromise" our ideals at times, but we do so when it is in the interest of having things work most effectively, so that our Vision and our Joy may be fulfilled.

## Exercise 1: Time Line for Your Vision

For this exercise, we will set our Vision on a time line. In the same way that it is easier to navigate through a maze when you begin at the end and work your way toward the beginning, we will start at the end of our Vision, the fulfillment of it, and work our way back to the present.

Begin by deciding when you would like to see your Vision fully realized. Let Joy, not fear, direct your answer. Your Vision should be big enough that it will take your lifetime to fulfill, and how long you live can be greatly determined by how much you have to live for. At the same time, don't let yourself be too limited by "realism"—you may not be able to go to the moon tomorrow, but with freedom from fear and the passion of Joy, you can indeed create miracles!

At the top of a new page in your Workbook, write "On my _____ birthday, . . ." Fill in the blank with the birthday by which you want to see your Vision being completely fulfilled. Then write down the components of your Vision as you created them in the last exercise of Chapter 7. Write them down in such a way that some action is taking place to let you know your Vision is being realized.

For example, let us say you want to create "educational opportunities for all people." Your Vision is to make this possible through a unique scholarship program where each recipient of a scholarship promises to help finance or raise the funds for two future recipients. Those two then help finance four future recipients (two each) and the scholarship mushrooms. On your hundredth birthday you will know that this Vision is being achieved as programs are being set up for this purpose around the world, and 10,000 people have already received an education.

Now go to ten years earlier and write down this new birthdate. Next to it, describe those things which would have to happen so that ten years later the Vision above is realized. For example: "On my ninetieth birthday, an international "Education for All" symposium will have convened for developing affordable education. Participants in the symposium will have committed to establishing the scholarship program in their country. A thousand people will have already received an education from the program started here."

Now go to ten years earlier and do the same thing. For example, "On my eightieth birthday, the 'Education for All' foundation I began at age fifty, working with area universities, will have gathered the necessary sponsors for an international symposium in ten years. We will have contacted the participants for the symposium, and they will already be starting their research into new models for affordable education. The scholarship fund I set up at age forty will have just received 100 new benefactors, previous recipients who will now help finance the way for other prospective students, and outreach efforts are bringing the program to major cities across the country."

Keep going to ten years earlier in this way until you come to ten years from your present age. (If working back ten years at a time does not bring you to exactly your present age, then go back to the number of years which will bring you to ten years from now. For example, if you are 52 years old and plan to live to 100, start at 100, go back to 90, 80, 70, and then to 62 years old, which is ten years from now.)

After writing down what you will be doing ten years from now, do the same thing for five years from now, then three years, two years, and one year. Next, go to six months from now, then three months, two months, and one month. Finally, fill in your time line for three weeks from now, then two weeks, and then one week.

Now, we have our goals for each week of the next month. When one month has passed, you will need to fill in the tasks to be done for each week of the next month, since the time line jumps from one to two months. Go to the tasks to be accomplished at the end of two months and work backward to the present one-month mark. Do the same when the second month has passed, then the third, and so on, so you always have your goals for the coming week.

In creating this structure, you are listening to Joy's Impulse. But that, of course, means you have to be willing to change the whole thing at a moment's notice, if Joy should tell you your Vision is better served in another way, or that it must evolve according to the need of a new moment. The Vision itself never changes, just the means to get there and the forms that the Joy of it will take. This is not a problem; as you work with this time line, getting familiar with the flow that it creates, you will not need to write it down, for it will take on a life of its own, writing and rewriting itself as you live it.

## Exercise 2: Putting Your Commitments into Action

It is essential, as we put our weekly commitments into action, to translate our abstract ideals into concrete form. If our commitments are about "feeling loving," "being nonjudgmental," or "expressing Joy," our understanding of what we are to actually be doing will quickly lapse into vagueness and we will have no sense of accomplishing our goals. Instead, we must find ways to objectify our ideals, giving them concrete substance, something we may look back upon and point to as we say, "Yes, I accomplished my goals for the week and here is the proof."

As you write your time line, then, make sure the goals you are writing down are concrete in this way. Again, the Vision itself may be pure ideal, abstract and unmeasurable, but for it to have meaning in our lives and make a difference in the world, it must wear a physical identity. Only in this way can we have solid actions to take as we walk through our fear into Joy.

There are three ways to accomplish this. First, when the goal is abstract, such as "forgiving someone" or "letting go of the fear of rejection," find some physical and measurable event that could not happen if you were still holding on to your grievance or your fear. For example, if you want to reach out to others in the fulfillment of your Vision but have a fear of rejection, then you might schedule a date to speak in public somewhere, risking the rejection and doing the opposite of what the fear said to do. If you want to stop being a people pleaser, always on call to meet others' needs and never your own, then risk some definite actions that fly in the face of others' demands, such as saying no to them, asking for something from them, or whatever actions call forth your fear of their abandonment. If it has a voice, a face, a place in time and space, if it is something you can point to and identify as a concrete event, then you have made it physical.

If you are still stuck on ideas for how to make your abstract goal concrete, such as the goal of letting go of worry or the need to control things to ensure a successful outcome, then you can either take the actions which risk failure, or simply notice when you are worrying and, using any of the exercises in the book, let go of the worry. This does not yet have a concrete marker, but if you then write down the experience of having let go of worry, in the act of writing it down you make it "real"; you mark it in time and space and know that a real transaction has occurred.

To make this more powerful, set out in advance with the goal that you will let go of worry, or whatever the task, three times a day for the week, or until it becomes a habit that you know will not dissolve when fear comes along. Carry a pad and pen with you to mark down the thoughts, feelings, and circumstances involved each time you do it. This "three times a day," or more if you choose, brings further specificity and concretization.

Review your time line and rewrite your goals as necessary with these principles in mind.

## Exercise 3: Declaring Your Vision

Now to build the structure that will carry us through any fears that would have us give up our commitments and our Vision. Hire a support person for the job. That is, ask someone to agree to have you report to them at the end of every day, or a couple of times a week, to go through an accounting of your work and how well you have kept to your commitments. When you have come up against some barrier to success, have them ask you the right questions, perhaps the questions of the core fear exercise, to discover the fear that is stopping you. Then, recommit to your goal, find a way to catch up with your time line, and assign to your support person the duty of making sure you do so.

It is essential at this point that you choose someone who will not allow his or her own fears to stop them from fulfilling his or her commitment to you. Make sure you are not giving yourself a way out by picking a support person who will let you get away with not fulfilling your commitments. Tell them that you are charging them with the task of caretaking your Vision, your highest aspirations, what is most important to you.

Next, begin declaring your Vision to others. This is not the same as reporting to your support person to make sure you reach your goals. Rather, it is a way of putting yourself into the arena of a public forum, where once having declared your Vision, it is expected you will make good on it. Others are looking to you now to keep your word and fulfill your promises. Your Vision cannot be so easily dropped as when it existed only in the privacy of your thoughts or between you and your support person.

In declaring your Vision to others, you are telling them that this is who you are, this is what you are all about, what you are devoting your life to. The Vision no longer lives just in your head but takes on life and reality in the telling. Others start to see you that way, assigning to you the meaning of "someone who is living his or her Vision." By making such declarations, you put yourself into action, compelled to fulfill your commitments, becoming inspired by your ability to make things happen and inspiring others to do the same.

## Exercise 4: Committing Yourself to Others

Finally, we lock ourselves into our Vision in a way that we cannot escape from. Begin to make commitments, in line with your Vision, that involve other people. Make promises to do things for them, such that they will become dependent upon you to fulfill your promises. Have them count on you for the realization of some goal of theirs that is in line with your Vision. To use the example of "education for all," you might promise to raise the funds to send them to college. Or in the interest of creating a more favorable work environment, you might promise to speak to the boss on behalf of those who are too afraid. By involving others in your commitments this way, they become the team that will fulfill your Vision with you.

Just as important, delegate various tasks of your Vision to the people you are making your promises to. Have them make commitments to you. Set it up so that you are interdependent upon each other for your now mutual Vision to be realized.

For instance, the person you have promised to send to college can promise in return to help finance two future recipients, speak to potential sponsors of the program, or help to recruit others who need educational assistance. They will have a great vested interest in the Vision as they do so, knowing what it is like not to have the opportunity for education and knowing as well all that an education makes possible. They will become powerful spokespeople, caretakers, living representatives of what the Vision is all about. In this way, they become equally invested in and responsible for bringing the Vision into reality.

This is systems theory; you are creating a system for generating the Vision. You set the system in motion by making promises to each other in the fulfillment of it. The Vision is bigger than any one person; it lives in the Joy of the interactions between people.

As you make your commitments to each other, include specific times when you'll fulfill these commitments. Get support people who will see to it that each of you makes and keeps these commitments. The support people also should be trained in how to help you if you begin to struggle with fear.

Beware! It is all too easy to let yourself slide if these structures are not in place. The long-standing habit of fear and defense will derail you in an instant if given a chance. Without this mechanism, it is unlikely we will make change.

There is another reason that making commitments to others and involving them with your Vision is so important. If you should somehow not complete your part, others have now taken on the Vision and will make sure your part gets fulfilled. The Vision has become a movement with a life of its own. It will be carried on beyond you, despite you, and you have surrendered your personal stake in it to give it to the cause of Joy.

This is the final and potentially most fearful part of our work. This is where it all gets very real. Be prepared for the fear that says if you commit yourself to others, they will come to demand too much of you. As we have seen, this is the fear of responsibility that belies the Joy of our task. In truth, you are never obligated to others, but for the sake of our Joy we want to become involved with them. The "responsibility" that comes with our Vision is the privilege of expressing our Joy in a way that serves.

Another fear comes up with the possibility of making your commitments to others and failing. This is the fear that they will be disappointed and withdraw their love as a result. Again, failure or success is not the name of the game. Rather, we want to practice listening to the prescription of Joy in the moment, facing our fear of others' disappointment that we will not comply with their attempts to control reality. Instead, we consider the "failure" as information from Joy on how to reorganize toward our goal.

Be aware also of the potential fear that your Vision might change form as others become involved; it was not yours to begin with and you don't want to try to control reality now. Know that you simply gave utterance to the expression of Joy that wanted to be lived, first through you and now through others, so that it may be born into the world for the benefit of all.

And remember, above all, as you take these final steps into a commitment that you cannot escape from, that fear is disappearing from our life and will ultimately have no place in your Vision. You are becoming free to live for Joy, for your heart's desire, for holy happiness. Be bold for Joy! We're not stopping now for fear's considerations of time, money, or the desire to "take it easy in life." We are not stopping for anything that would keep us from the commitment to our highest Vision, to what we have always wanted with all of our heart, to our Purpose and our very Life. This is the time. Today is the appointed day for you to start seeing the world around you transform and you with it! Today is the appointed day to begin living in radical Joy!

# EPILOGUE

The principles laid out in this book are addressed to you, the individual. Each of us lives in the world of our own perception, adopting a core fear and chief defense that project out as the stories of our lives. We develop a personality that responds to these projections in its unique way, with more or less success in creating Joy.

Entire countries and cultures develop personalities along these same principles. In its negative aspect, this gives birth to a Hitler or Hussein, who draw their power by playing on the fears and defenses of the culture. When the cultural identity or "personality" of a country is threatened with a loss of power or independence, they respond with a particular defense style, according to the perception given by their core fear. The leader becomes a figurehead for this defense—often, literally, the chief in charge of the defense. Stirring up the fears of the people, they invoke a call to separation, a nationalism that says fighting the enemy (really, the core fear) for the survival of the country is worth dying for.

In its positive aspect, we see leaders such as Gandhi, King, Lincoln, and Mandela, who have transformed the politics of separation into a higher ideal. Inclusiveness, emancipation, nonviolent and nonfearful resistance are the hallmarks of a power which cannot be threatened by fear. FDR's statement acknowledges this: "The only thing we have to fear is fear itself."

As the world becomes smaller and smaller, the physical barriers to Oneness being minimized through technology, our failure to keep pace psychologically has devastating consequences. More and more the world is embracing the ways of Western, particularly American, culture. "The American experiment" was built on an idealism that would transcend the fears and defenses imposed by England. It would provide a religious tolerance and freedom of thinking that was inclusive, not separatist.

But this is now being distorted throughout the world, with disastrous results, by a chief defense of *needing* to be independent. Independence can be a wonderful thing, but when it turns compulsive, driven by a fear that is out of control, it is no longer a testimony to freedom but to slavery. We *must* be independent and cannot choose a healthy dependence, or interdependency, when called for. We *must* have our own property and our own ways—"I did it my way" and the "me" generation are but examples. As a result, our families fall apart, we fail to make necessary commitments and exercise appropriate discipline to work for what is valuable. We suffer the great epidemic of our society called loneliness and isolation. And we fail to consider the effect of our actions on others, perceiving them as threats to our independence and our "right to have."

Ultimately, the entire world is driven by the core fear of returning to Oneness, losing our independence, our individuality, and giving up our "freedom of choice." In exercising our chief defense we try to control reality, to arrange it as we please, asserting our autonomy and power. This has tragic consequences: the rape of the earth, where we take what we want without regard for our dependence on all life; the threat of nuclear annihilation, where we would assert our power over all things to the point of complete destruction; and on and on the list goes.

The politics of separation, the attempt to be powerful *over* anything, must yield to a humble recognition of our interdependence and Oneness. It will no longer do to impose our individual wishes upon others and upon reality. We must accept our rightful place in the natural order of things if we want to create a new way of being.

Each time a group of people (two or more gathering together in Joy's Name) agrees to let go of fear and embrace Joy, they create a new perception. As enough of us live in this new perception a consensus reality is established, one with the power to carry others along who are still clinging to old ways. Our greatest responsibility, therefore, is to practice the principles of Joy for ourselves and to join with others as we do so. Only in this can we change the balance of forces in the world. Only in this can we open up the living experience of "a better way." Only in this can we usher in a world that works, a world of Oneness, Harmony, Beauty, and Joy.

# SUGGESTIONS FOR FURTHER READING

Bach, Richard, *Illusions: The Adventures of a Reluctant Messiah*, Dell 1994.

Campbell, Joseph, *The Power of Myth*, Anchor Books, 1991.

Carpenter, Tom, *Dialogue on Awakening: Communion with Jesus*, Carpenter Press, 1996.

Castaneda, Carlos, *The Teachings of Don Juan: A Yaqui Way of Knowledge*, California Academy of Sciences, 1998.

Frankl, Victor, *Man's Search for Meaning*, Beacon Press, 1998.

Gibran, Kahlil, *The Prophet*, Knopf, 1995.

Jung, C. G., *Memories, Dreams and Reflections*, Vintage, 1989.

Millman, Dan, *Way of the Peaceful Warrior*, Kramer, 1985.

Morgan, Marlo, *Mutant Message Down Under,* HarperCollins, 1995.

Rodegast, Pat, *Emmanuel's Book: A Manual for Living Comfortably in the Cosmos,* Bantam, 1987.

Rumi, Jellaludin, *Rumi: In the Arms of the Beloved,* translated by Jonathan Star, Tarcher/Putnam, 1997.

Thoreau, Henry David, *Walden,* Vintage, 1998.

And for those interested in *A Course in Miracles:*

*A Course in Miracles Text, Workbook for Students, Manual for Teachers* (combined edition), Viking, 1996.

*A Course in Miracles: What It Says,* Kenneth Wapnick and Helen Schucman, Penguin Audiobooks, 1996.

Tuttle, Paul Norman, *Conversations with Raj* (a newsletter, published by Northwest Foundation for "A Course in Miracles," P.O. Box 1490, Kingston, WA 98346).

Made in United States
North Haven, CT
10 December 2021

12325434R00159